# ART SCENES
## THE SOCIAL SCRIPTS OF THE ART WORLD

PABLO HELGUERA

# ART SCENES
## THE SOCIAL SCRIPTS OF THE ART WORLD

Jorge Pinto Books
New York

*Art Scenes: The Social Scripts of the Art World*

© 2012 Pablo Helguera

All rights reserved. This book may not be reproduced in whole or in part, in any form (beyond copying permitted by Sections 107 and 108 of the United States Copyright Law, and except limited excerpts by reviewer for the public press), without written permission from Jorge Pinto Books Inc., Bethesda, MD, 20816. jpinto@mac.com.

Edition © 2012 Jorge Pinto Books Inc.

ISBN: 978-1-934978-99-3
ISBN10: 1-934978-99-X

Edited by Rebecca Roberts.

Design: Charles King: www.ckmm.com

Cover illustration © 2012 Pablo Helguera

# Contents

Acknowledgments . . . . . . . . . . . . . . . . . . . . *ix*

I: Introduction:
   (An Outline for Art World Studies) . . . . . . . . 1
II: Theater of Values
   . . . . . . . . . . . . . . . . . . . . . . . . 13
III: We Are the Art
   (The Birth of the Art Scene) . . . . . . . . . . 23
IV: The Disruptive Character:
   The Artistic Script . . . . . . . . . . . . . . . 41
V: The Regulating Character:
   The Academic Script . . . . . . . . . . . . . . . 53
VI: Distribution, Discourse, and Subsidiary
   Scripts . . . . . . . . . . . . . . . . . . . . . 71
VII: Rewriting the Script:
   The Rise of the Art User . . . . . . . . . . . . 87
VIII: Alternate Endings:
   (The Art Scene Doubled) . . . . . . . . . . . . . 95

Appendices . . . . . . . . . . . . . . . . . . . . . 101

Alternative Time and Instant Audience:
   (The Public Program as an Alternative Space)   103
Variations on an Audience . . . . . . . . . . . . . 117
Other Titles by the Author . . . . . . . . . . . . . 125

# Acknowledgments

This book is the result of my doctoral research work at the faculty of Art, Design and Architecture of Kingston University in London. I am deeply grateful to Catherine McDermott for her constant support and encouragement in developing this work. I am thankful also to Fran Lloyd, Jane Nobbs, the faculty at Kingston, and their students, and to Sally Tallant and Felicity Allen, who were also key advisors and interlocutors to this project. I am thankful as always to Wendy Woon, Director of Education at The Museum of Modern Art, New York, as well as my colleagues in the Education Department there, for their continued support and collective reflections on our many experiments in the galleries and public programs, which have nurtured many of the ideas here. I also had the pleasure of working with art historian James Elkins in organizing a symposium entitled Art Speech at MoMA in May 2011, which helped inform some of the thoughts presented in chapter five of this book. Last but not least, I want to thank a few artist friends and colleagues with whom I share common conversations and interests on this subject: Caroline Woolard, Paul Ramirez Jonas, Morgan J. Puett, and Amy Whitaker, a fellow writer and inspiring thinker, who generously provided her feedback to this work.

# INTRODUCTION

## (AN OUTLINE FOR ART WORLD STUDIES)

Art makes us perform.

   This is not a comment on how we become motivated to make performance art. Instead, I mean to say that the social environment constructed around art leads to a particular kind of conduct among those exposed to it. This conduct is manifested in formal and informal ways—ranging from conversations and subtle social interactions to formal presentations that can be academic or simply promotional; they can be merely intuitive or highly calculated. We make art in a particular social context, it becomes enveloped in an art world, and that, in turn, influences our behavior. So, to elaborate on my initial statement: artists make art that creates an art world that makes all of us who belong to that world perform. And, as we perform, we contribute to the construction of an art scene.

The main premise of this book is that contemporary art makes us perform self-conscious or instinctive interpretive acts; and that the construction of value in artworks is determined less by the objects themselves than by the nature of our interpretive performances, having a trickle-down effect on practically every aspect of art in society.

This book aims to contribute in a small way to the neglected field of the sociology of contemporary art. The sociology of art has historically focused on the examination of how visual art becomes the expression of a particular historical period—that is, how art represents the ideas of the society that produced it. A less-studied subject is the sociology of today's art world: how those who become invested in art also become both contributors to it and the social product of it and express themselves using its vocabulary. In the twenty-first century, there is a developed, global, highly professionalized and vast cultural class that governs the way in which art is produced, interpreted, and disseminated. It is becoming more and more important to gain a better understanding of this loose social network that lives and communicates through the collectively constructed values it presents to the world.

While art historians and academics study concrete periods of art or artists whose work enacts a social critique of their environment, they often shy away from the sociology of art itself. With the desire to explore that gap, starting in the mid-nineties I published articles—mostly of a satirical nature—commenting on the foibles and contradictions of the art world.* This initial interest developed further as part of my work as a museum educator and organizer of public programs in various art institutions, where I observed and reflected on the behavior of both art professionals and amateurs. It eventually became apparent to me that what had, at first, seemed a curiosity was in fact a serious matter of study, as I began realizing how social dynamics condition our thinking and learning. This eventually drew me to socially engaged art and to the promotion of the creation of a new field of research that I have sometimes described as "art world studies." This small book is the result of these ongoing reflections, and it is presented with the hope that it will help initiate a discussion about social behavior within the art world.

Another goal for this project is to show that the default perspective from which the society of art is currently analyzed—namely, the financial angle—is very narrow. Although it may appear counterintuitive to some, this book departs from the belief that the art market's role in the valuation process of art is actually dependent on social processes that are themselves not always dependent on the art market; which is another way of saying that, while the art market may have an impact on how certain kinds of art are valued, and while it can serve as a barometer of sorts regarding what kinds of art are gaining traction in certain circles, it generally functions more like an imperfect

---

\* My first article on the art world ("The Opening Game: A Guide to the Art World's Favorite Ritual Pastime") was published in *Chicago Artists' News* (the Chicago Artists' Coalition newsletter) in May 1997 (p. 7).

mirror of a priori processes of valuation that obey other forces, and it most definitely does not always represent, nor accurately reflect, the thoughts and interests of the art world as a whole. It most certainly does not account for the "non-economic" economy of art—which includes emerging fields and art supported by academic circuits, social and political organizations, nonprofit organizations, co-ops, educational institutions, individually funded art enterprises with very specific focuses, foundations, and government programs, among many others; nor does it represent art scenes in cities or countries that have scant or no commercial galleries, in places like the Middle East, Africa, South America, or Asia. It can't absorb many of the new and important cross-disciplinary trends that actively dialogue with the vocabulary and concerns of contemporary art, which include technology, sciences, and the humanities, and that instead of producing objects tend to emphasize experiential works that are difficult to insert into the art market. And, last but not least, there is a growing group of artists all over the world whose work is specifically about creating alternative economies that counter the art market, finding other sources of sustainability—art microsystems designed specifically to not be co-opted by the conventional world of art fairs or galleries. In sum, there are vast numbers of artists and institutions globally that exist largely under the art market's radar, that have little to no relationship to the world of galleries, and that produce and support art under very different circumstances and interests, a lot of which is eventually recognized by international exhibitions and publications.

These many important developments in art most definitely are having an effect in the art market—for example, by inspiring market-friendly works by other artists—but to think that the art market is dictating or even documenting the development of these many other branches of art practice is misguided. Most of the time, the art market is a good barometer of nothing other than itself.

There certainly is something very seductive about looking at the art world from the money side. The backdoor dealing, the veils of privacy, the issues of provenance and authenticity, the eccentricity shown in the purchase of dubious goods, as well as the sums of money that are exchanged and the colorful characters that participate in this world: in the hands of a good writer, these make for a juicy and entertaining read. This probably accounts for the popularity of books such as *The $12 Million Stuffed Shark: The Curious Economics of Contemporary Art*, by Don Thompson (Palgrave Macmillan, 2008), and Sarah Thornton's *Seven Days in the Art World* (W.W. Norton & Co., 2009), both of which provide a glimpse into the inner dynamics of contemporary art society, mainly through economics—selling, collecting, and the status attained through those processes.*

The economics of the art world gets so much attention that there is a whole small industry of discussion circles

---

\* Several other magazines and blogs, such as ArtWorld Salon, a leisurely blog of various art professionals (to which I contribute as editor), also normally gravitate toward economic issues. For several years I have also contributed editorial cartoons for *The Art Newspaper*, probably the most reliable international publication specializing in reporting about the economics of the art world.

around it. Art fairs regularly feature panel discussions about collecting, and magazines report on the subject regularly (not least because art fairs, galleries, auction houses, and the like are their main advertising clients). It is therefore not surprising that whenever the mainstream media reports on contemporary art, it usually tends to fixate on the market. Yet it is remarkable how little there is to say about the subject. The many panels on collecting tend to be indistinguishable from one another, as they often deal with recurring topics; art fairs and their events are extremely repetitive and usually inconsequential, mainly affirming existing values.

Perhaps the most important reason why the art market is not an accurate indicator of the process of valuation is that it is largely focused on (or, better said, invested in) the material object. Yet the art object is not what it used to be. Thanks to factors such as the huge proliferation of art, the endless supply and production—due to fast and cheap production technology—that result in vast collections of thousands of objects, and the influence of conceptualism, which has gradually made the original seem more or less expendable, the art world has come to resemble the fashion industry. In that sense, art objects, even when they are considered masterpieces, are, for better or worse, manipulated placeholders for the ideas and reputations of the characters of the art world—the artists, those who curate and collect their work, and others.

I present this book out of my belief that in order to understand why certain ideas in art take precedence over others, there needs to be a better effort to grasp the way in which social, political, and philosophical concerns in the art of our time are negotiated in relation to the economic interests of the art world. In order to gain this better understanding, it is important to acknowledge that value in art is not an exclusive construct of the market, but the result of a complex web of debates that include political and theoretical exchanges, shifts in the historical moment, institutional and commercial promotion, and, of course, the emergence of thought-provoking art that pushes the discussion in a particular direction. The art world is a highly social environment that produces a close-knit network of art scenes (which I describe here as small performative environments), and it is essential to understand how those social interactions contribute to the negotiation among our different art values.

The social interactions of this highly specialized world, which I will refer to as "social scripts," are mostly conveyed through patterns of spoken communication and other subtle social codes, and they range in their degree of regimentation. As in much of society, the art world is surprisingly consistent; it follows set collective patterns of social exchange, as can be easily seen in the conventions that regulate the social events of most of its institutions—the art fair, the international biennial, the gallery environment, etc. These dynamics have been exacerbated by the growth of the art world into a professionalized arena with a seemingly never-endingly proliferating market of art and ideas. This unregulated proliferation is loosely managed by a network of tastemakers, in both academic and commercial areas of art, who reflect, exhibit, collect, and, mainly, communicate with each other to get a collective sense of what things are relevant to think about and how to respond to them.

Most would agree that we have long abandoned the time when we saw art as part of an inevitable "evolution," or as a relatively ordered debate around more or less established aesthetic and political opposites (Ingres vs. Delacroix, abstraction vs. representation, formalism vs. political art, etc.). The myriad forms, approaches, and styles of art today, as well as the overwhelming amount of work produced each day and the immediacy to which news of it comes to us, make it virtually impossible for us to think about art as we did even a few decades ago. Instead of maintaining the sense that we are participating in a historical continuum linked to the art of the past, we appear to participate in a loose threading of ever-fleeting present moments, one immediately contradicting the next. Even when a major biennial or exhibition opens, by the next day it belongs to the remote past and we are already thinking forward to the next defining event—even if that event will only be "defining" as fleetingly as the previous was. Our sense of existence within the art system closely relates to what Francisco de Quevedo once described as *"presentes sucesiones de difunto"*—present successions of dead people. In the art world, in our insatiable search for the new and the meaningful, we live among present successions of soon-to-be passé art.

Thrown as we are into an uncertain context that is too diverse, fluid, and varied to retain any semblance of cohesion, in making and discussing art we rely on our partial knowledge of present events, but increasingly we rely more on our intuition, on the collective assessments of those around us whose opinion we respect the most, and perhaps more importantly, on the social landscape against which a certain kind of art is starting to become meaningful (for example, when attending an exhibition where we already are somewhat familiar with some of the artists but not fully convinced of their worth, to encounter people we respect who are enthusiastic about the show can be a way to positively affirm our interest in it). This process is crucial because it lies at the core of what gives meaning to art today: the collective construction of value through agreement on taste and ideas, particularly among those who influence trends through their endorsement. Any understanding of the social dynamics of the art world needs to depart from this premise. I thus start this book by discussing value.

It lies beyond the scope of this book to offer a sociological theory of the art world in any way. I openly admit that, not being an anthropologist or sociologist by training, the task of conducting a qualitative study to verify some of the observations made in this book exceeds my abilities. I do hope, however, that the observations that I have made over the course of many years in the fields of art, education, and performance and the interpretations and conclusions I provide may be of help to future research. I have attempted to provide a schematic sense of what characterizes these dynamics and how I perceive them to operate, with the hope that this may prove sufficient to persuade others to engage in further research into this subject.

I would like to conclude with a few additional remarks: the book makes reference to the evolving role of the audience/participant, as well as the problem of creating a true alternativity that could rewrite socially constructed paradigms in art. Yet, because the narrative focus of the book is more on the process of construction of value, and it's not possible to elaborate on these other subjects, I felt it appropriate to add two earlier texts that address those subtopics in some way (see Appendices), the first on how we could go about rethinking the "alternative" in art by placing greater emphasis on time rather than space ("Alternative Time and Instant Audience [The Public Program as an Alternative Space]") and the second on how our performance should have sociolinguistic considerations ("Variations on an Audience").

Next, I imagine that some readers may interpret the main argument of this book to boil down to the simplistic point that we all are actors in society, and that art is only a reflection of that self-evident fact. My objective, however, is to indicate how this process of enacting responses to ideas and self-perceived relationships between oneself and others contributes to the construction of the social scores that ultimately create value and influence the course of events in art at a macroscopic scale. This construction of the performed "art scene" sets the primary framework for the creation of a society, and the study of this framework could be the basis and primary focus of the social anthropology of contemporary art, or art world studies.

Last but not least, the approach taken in this book may generate the impression that my general argument, permeated by the analogy of theater, turns artworks into mere props and exhibition spaces into mere sets. It is certainly not my intention to minimize the relevance of the art object nor to overlook the importance of physical environments in the construction of value. Instead, it is my belief that if we are going to build a sociology of the contemporary art world, it can't be centered on objects but on people and their social rituals around those objects. This is the message conveyed by most of the experimental works produced since the 1960s: if the art object has been slowly dematerializing, what takes its place is the social context around it.

My hope is that gaining a better insight into why we perform as we do in relation to art can both help us develop a greater critical perspective on how we set our views about today's art and also help us with the yet-unfinished modernist project of integrating art-making into other spheres of knowledge and experience.

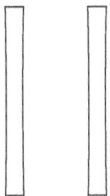

## THEATER OF VALUES

Given that this book examines the construction of value by discussing our performance around objects, it is necessary to start by briefly addressing the problematic nature of valuation when we use the art object as the departure point. It is mainly a distinction between intrinsic value—a favorite leitmotif of the art market—and extrinsic value in art.

Intrinsic value is one of the old problems of philosophy: is there something intrinsically valuable in an object (in our case, an artwork) that determines a range of reactions to it, or is the value we assign to objects entirely subjective? Certainly, when we collect and preserve artworks we operate on the basis that objects in themselves have some kind of intrinsic value. It is also problematic to declare that an art object doesn't have inherent characteristics that may affect a subjective valuation: how else can we explain why some objects produce continuous fascination throughout history, while others don't (i.e., why we have so consistently ruled, for example, that Rembrandt was the best artist of his time, as opposed to any other Dutch artist of that period)? So it is possible to argue that attributes of art objects produce a more or less consistent range of subjective responses. But the debate on objective and subjective value enters a dark territory after that, mostly because we can't definitively agree on whether an artwork has any permanent attributes (outside of its physical components, *if* it has physical components) that make it valuable to a given society at any given point in time. Particularly problematic (and this is a classic problem of art interpretation) is that we cannot satisfactorily explain why a given artwork can capture the interest of many people and yet provoke different and sometimes contrasting responses.

Pragmatists of the school of John Dewey would argue that it is misguided to search for an answer in any sort of permanent, abstract notion, because the world is constantly evolving. Instead, they would argue, we are better off learning from previous manifestations of the problem and the resolutions arrived at by others; so, in the case of art, we can only learn about it in relation to previous interpretations of what art means and by an analysis of how certain artworks affected that understanding. The neopragmatist Richard Rorty, who went further in the linguistic realm, was skeptical of abstract attributes that bear no concrete relation with specific situations; thus, he might have argued, there is no point in searching for a "true" value in an artwork because that quest ultimately has no bearing on how we conduct our business in real life (in real life we can only make judgments based on concrete examples not predetermined definitions of value; the latter would be a frustrating exercise, as contemporary artists have the special ability of constantly surprising us by making works that contradict any previous assumptions about what great or interesting art is).

While we can pretty quickly get deeply entangled in trying to define the intrinsic value of art or determine the intrinsic value of any given artwork, it is much easier to determine art's extrinsic value, by observing the processes enacted around the work in innumerable scenarios. For example, we know the specific effects that certain artworks have had on certain people, the exact conversations or debates they have triggered, and the innovations they have brought in subject matter or materials.

Furthermore, while objects lie at the center of the intrinsic-value debate, people are the enactors of extrinsic value, as it belongs to the realm of the subjective—a word that literally means "based on or influenced by personal feelings, tastes, or opinions."

With this in mind, I would like to set aside the question of intrinsic value, with the understanding that even if it does exist there would be no way for us to determine exactly what it is and, most importantly, because knowing it wouldn't have a bearing on our understanding of the creation of extrinsic value, in any case. Instead, I will discuss how extrinsic value is constructed, attempt to point out patterns, and how I see these patterns conforming to particular social scripts.

Now that we have distinguished between intrinsic and extrinsic value, it is necessary to establish what we mean by "extrinsic value" in art and the process by which this value is determined. Although it may not surprise most art world insiders, the fact that some art that garners high prices on the art market is not necessarily critically acclaimed or influential continues to be a confounding aspect of the art world. Similarly, it is still not easy to explain why many artworks—and artists—carry significant reputational value that is not directly reflected in the price tag the work has in the art market. This may be due to the fact that the works are intangible, ephemeral, no longer existing, not easy to collect (such as a lot of conceptual and process-based art) or, in contrast, too easily distributable. John Cage's oeuvre, for instance, one of the most influential of the twentieth century, does not comprise many objects (since he was primarily a composer), but none of the objects Cage did make garner the prices achieved by the paintings of some of his contemporaries. This example shows (aside from the fact that the art market is a poor assessor of the importance of certain artists or ideas) that valuation in art cannot be studied from a single angle; it is social interactions that establish a dialogue between critical and economic valuation.

Second, the generalized perception (mostly by people outside the art world) that the values of artworks and artists are directed or controlled by a small art elite is too simplistic to accurately represent the complex web of processes that take a work to the level of visibility that results in many top art institutions collecting it and top scholars becoming interested in studying it. This is more true in the twenty-first century than ever before: sixty years ago, long before the proliferation of international biennials, art fairs, and similar vehicles, the power of taste-making resided with a relatively small group of individuals and institutions. For instance, it would be hard for us today to point out an individual with the influence over the course of art that Alfred H. Barr, the founding director of New York's Museum of Modern Art, once had. Today the art world is so vast and its pace so frenetic that no single entity has that degree of clout; in the art world of today, collective consensus in a wide number of contexts and moments has become essential.

Furthermore, what moves the conversation forward in the art world, unlike in a scientific community, is never an objectively verifiable contribution such as the discovery of a vaccine or the solution to a mathematical problem. Instead, those works or ideas considered the most dominant or relevant in art today are those that provoke—or that we believe provoke—a certain type of conversation or reassessment of the current state of affairs in art discourse or in the world. An artwork or an artist emerges against a background of debates among many people. Those discussions adjudicate value and single individuals out from the universe of art.

There are three important things to note about this process of construction of value:

The first is the extent to which the process is dependent on collective communication—which includes critical writing, public events, marketing, and, most importantly, word-of-mouth assessments and socializing. This is why, like the trade shows and conventions of other industries, biennials, art fairs, and large-scale exhibitions are key places for the creation of favorable or unfavorable public opinion about an artist's work. The more an artist or a work generates conversation, the more likely it is that they will eventually be considered representative of the period.

The second is that this process does not follow a set logic or rationale and can, in fact, be fairly unpredictable, as it results from a combination of factors, ranging from the visibility of a given artist and issue in the field to the accidental historic and economic moment, which may promote a search for a particular kind of artist. For example, with the recent surge of biennials in the Middle East and the momentous civil movements taking place in the region simultaneously, it has become pressing in the art world to find artists who can speak to that reality from an informed, perhaps even firsthand standpoint. Curators today are careful not to fall into the geographic determinism that characterized some of the first major global biennials in the period after the fall of the Berlin Wall, but, at the same time, there continues to be a certain expectation that such exhibitions will have a degree of international presence.

The third has to do with recognizable narratives, which I also term social or art historical scripts. These, in their crudest form, are very visible in the art market, where the tried-and-true formulas of well-known artists are emulated by lesser-known, less original artists. A "second-tier" market of work by such artists is supported by dealers and collectors who can't acquire the work of first-tier artists; the work is usually not explicitly termed or acknowledged as second-tier but rather described as "alternative" or "in the line of."

In a more sophisticated formulation of this recognizable narrative, we are in a constant search for the "next Warhol," the "next Bruce Nauman," and so forth: not simply imitators but artists who have created alternate bodies of work which, even though they may differ formally and even conceptually from their forebears, feature an *equivalent narrative*. The success with which this biographical arc is communicated determines the entrance of the artist's work into the art historical canon and, as a result, its consideration for collections, "canonical" narratives, and such.*

These three characteristics of value construction (consensus through communication, nonobjective analysis, and the recognition of familiar narratives) are deeply linked to both performance and interpretation. Independently of the reasons why a work is deemed extraordinary (i.e., as having great intrinsic value), for it to be meaningful (i.e., acquire extrinsic value) it is crucial for it to perform successfully in those three aspects of the social realm of art. This performance is usually the responsibility of the artist, but it also falls to those who advocate for the work (be it a gallery or a curator or critic who is invested in the work). In the terms of idealist philosophy, *esse est percipi* (to be is

---

* The press is eager to find and proclaim various emerging artists as the inheritors of the role played by previous well-known artists. For example, see Ariel Levy's article "Warhol's Children," in *Time Out New York*, January 15, 2007, pp. 20–1.

to be perceived); if a work doesn't manage to penetrate the critical discourse and show up on the art world's radar, it stands little chance of having a meaningful impact on it.

The previously enumerated characteristics of how art is collectively valued may provide contemporary art skeptics with ammunition to prove that art is little more than a capricious conversation elevated to a high realm. This, as I will discuss in chapter five of this book, is a valid critique. But, briefly, the problem with it is that it presupposes that the process of the construction of value in art is, or should be, organized and methodical, an ongoing balancing of the books. The root of the perception that the art world is whimsically arbitrary is the idea that art should "perform" for us—as opposed to us performing for it, as I am trying to argue. Similar to a rational/totalitarian state that attempts to determine what must happen or not happen, historical attempts to make art follow a particular course (such as government art programs, official art, etc.) have yielded poor results, producing either overly academic, overly didactic, or instrumentalized work that leaves little to no interpretive or experiential space to the audience. (This is an important subject that has acquired even more relevance with the emergence of socially engaged art—art that has as its primary objective the construction of a collective experience *as* art. In chapter eight of this book I will argue that this new set of practices helps address the problem of the performative interpretation of art and discuss the way this interpretation adjudicates value.) So, the short response to this critique of the valuations of the art world as arbitrary and whimsical is that it is misguided to expect the art world to behave rationally, as it is not built to operate that way. The art world, instead, adjudicates the extrinsic values of different artists and artworks in response to the interests, needs, and interests of a particular moment, the result of intangible rounds of collective assessments performed within an art scene that allow it to focus on those works that it eventually will deem most representative, and remarkable, for their time.

This would be the best way to explain the theater of consumption of art,* where there are so many of us making, exhibiting, speaking, blogging, and tweeting about art at every minute that it is impossible to see it or synthesize it all. We are left to construct representative "art scenes"—small collective projects that are nothing but our performed, provisional, and interpretive reading of what is happening—usually making an effort to position ourselves at the center of the story.

I will therefore attempt to characterize some of the main types of "scripts" that are performed: today's entrepreneurial construct of the artist, the script of academia and its attendant patterns, and the emerging script of the audience as "art users" and its relationship with socially engaged art—all of these influenced by the pivotal roles of marketing or distribution and of collective conversation, or discourse, as a script-building mechanism.

---

* I take the term "theater of consumption of art" from A. Fuat Firat and Nikhilesh Dholakia's book *Consuming People: From Political Economy to Theaters of Consumption* (New York and London: Routledge, 1999).

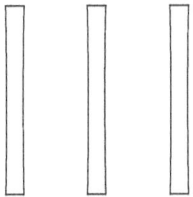

# WE ARE THE ART
## (THE BIRTH OF THE ART SCENE)

*Encubre a tus hermanos el amor que les tengas y disimula tus pasiones ante los hombres, porque eres, hijo mío, un mal actor de tus emociones.*\*

—Julio Torri, *De Fusilamientos* (1914)

In order to understand the performative parameters of the art scene today it is necessary to review a number of art historical terms, debates, and ideas around the art world and around social behavior in general that emerged sometime around the 1960s.

In 1964, Arthur Danto famously described the conditions in which an artwork would ideally be understood: "An

---

\* "Hide your love from your brethren and fake your passions before men, because you are, my son, a bad actor of your emotions."

atmosphere of artistic theory, a history of art: an artworld."*
This social environment, composed of people at various levels of initiation and investment in art, is relevant here because of its role as clearinghouse of taste and influence for the mainstream, both through formal (pedagogical, academic) and informal (fashion, commerce) channels. Contemporary art is dependent on the atmosphere Danto describes in order to be validated and supported intellectually and commercially through these channels.

A few years after Danto's essay was published, a new term gradually emerged in the daily lexicon of contemporary art: *art scene*. At least two books in the 1960s used the term in their titles: *New York: The New Art Scene*, by Alan R. Solomon, in 1967, and *The Art Scene*, by Barrie Sturt-Penrose, in 1969.

While *artworld*, as originally used by Danto, refers to an intellectual context that gives meaning to things, *art scene*, by contrast, as reflected by the above-mentioned works and subsequent uses of the term in other publications, always refers to something less impregnated by an artistic theory, more determined by the forces of the market, and decidedly more sexy: a fashionable arena or playing field where art may be the magnet, but the predominant idea is "to see and be seen"; in other words, an environment where there are admired objects, but the main objective is tied to social relations.

The appropriateness of this descriptor was clearly demonstrated in 1965. That year, Andy Warhol's retrospective

---

* Arthur Danto, "The Artworld," *The Journal of Philosophy* 61, no. 19 (Oct. 15, 1964): 580.

famously opened in Philadelphia, and attendance in the galleries was such that the paintings had to be taken down for safety. Warhol and his collaborators were greeted by a hysterical mass of adoring fans, unaware or uninterested in the fact that the gallery walls were empty. As Warhol himself said of the incident, "We weren't just at the art exhibit, we were the exhibit, we were the art incarnate."\*

Clearly, there was an art scene in turn-of-the century Vienna, in Paris in the teens, and in 1950s New York. Yet, the period of the 1960s marks a paradigm shift, an increased awareness of the influence of the context around an artwork, that is illustrated by the Warhol anecdote. Much as this social event that entirely and effectively displaced the artwork or, rather, placed it in the experience of meeting the artist, process art emerged in that period with the goal of displacing the art object.

Parenthetically, I would like to propose that the "incarnation of art" that Warhol was alluding to connects with yet another term that emerged in the art criticism of the period: that is, "theatricality." It was most visibly introduced in 1967, in another art historically ubiquitous essay, by Michael Fried. "Art and Objecthood"†—which unsuspectingly laid the theoretical groundwork for Minimalism—made as its central argument the idea that the works discussed provoked an extreme self-consciousness that resulted in theatricality. As those familiar with sixties art theory know, Fried's essay has led to a number

---

\* Andy Warhol and Pat Hackett, *Popism: The Warhol Sixties* (Boston: Mariner Books: 1980), p. 132.
† Michael Fried, *Art and Objecthood: Essays and Reviews*. Chicago: University of Chicago Press, 1998, p. 148.

of critical responses regarding the nature of Minimalism and the questions it presented to modernism and, in a more ancillary manner, what we mean by "theatricality." In the view of Stephen Melville, who in a lecture discussed Fried's notion of theatricality in detail, the essay is a Kantian attempt to critique a work that is unable to simply "be" but instead attempts to publicly address itself and actively involve the public in that tautology—a critique that ultimately fails, Melville argues, because it is highly subjective:

> It is, finally, an argument about the kinds of beings we are and about the intertwining of our ability to acknowledge others with our capacity for expression, and thus also about our deep—ontological, Fried would say—obligation to experience.*

Fried's use of "theatrical" then—which, Melville points out, is similar to "mannered"—carried, and continues to carry, certain negative connotations. We use the words "contrived" or "didactic" when we experience a work that is attempting, perhaps a bit too hard, to promote a particular line of thinking that is not self-critical or that may be perceived as self-righteous. What Fried does introduce in his essay, and which is very relevant to our understanding of what happened when Warhol entered that gallery opening in Philadelphia and saw himself as the art, is the notion that there is an operation of postmodern self-awareness

---

* Stephen Melville, *"Art and Objecthood": A Lecture*, in the series *Quaderns Portatils* (Barcelona: MACBA, 2007), p. 14.

taking place: as Michel Foucault wrote of *Las Meninas*, "a slender line of reciprocal visibility embraces a whole complex network of uncertainties, exchanges, and feints,"* or, in other words, a process of "perceiving yourself perceiving"—a Robert Irwin phrase†—which informs practically all post-Minimalist art. From this perspective, Fried's essay (likely to his disappointment) affirms the idea that, once we have gained the consciousness of seeing ourselves from the outside, there is no going back. As in Novalis's famous quote, "We are near waking when we dream that we dream." In other words, once we discover our theatricality, once we get rid of the fourth wall, it is impossible to act without the awareness that it is there.

Because of the context in which it has been used historically, the term *art scene* has always carried a somewhat frivolous connotation—less in relation to the intellectual environment referred to by Danto than to the convening places of the Warholian, fashion-friendly crowd. But, more important for our purposes, whereas today's term *art world* refers more to the global network of the profession, *art scene* refers more specifically to a location on a smaller scale, such as a city or neighborhood; being more concrete, it suggests a mise-en-scène in which the real-life drama of art unfolds. In other words, when the social process meets art-making, locality becomes stage, and those who enter

---

\* Michel Foucault, *The Order of Things*. (New York: Routledge, 2001) p. 4.
† Olafur Eliasson and Robert Irwin, "Take Your Time: A Conversation," in *Take your time: Olafur Eliasson*, Madeleine Grynsztejn, ed. (San Francisco: San Francisco Museum of Modern Art; London: Thames & Hudson, 2007), pp. 51–61 (exh. cat.).

it have no other choice but to engage in it as spectators or as actors. The emergence of the term *art scene* is not simply the result of a time in history in which a number of important social components collided to create a remarkable moment in art—that could be said of many periods in history. The term is fitting because, along with the works that emerged starting in the early sixties, artists developed that acute, theatrical, historical self-consciousness that led them to address their own role as "actors" in the unfolding art historical play before them.

But if we agree that the art scene is the local set of the play, who are, then, the actors? To answer this question it is useful to turn to the work of yet another of the few thinkers who took the time to reflect on the world of art—a sociologist.

In 1982, Howard S. Becker published *Art Worlds*, part of his effort to contribute to the sociology of art, a field that he considered overlooked. In his book (which addresses all the arts, not only visual art) Becker emphasizes the collective process of production, distribution, and interpretation of art, breaking away from the stereotype of the isolated genius to show how art is supported by a complex web of collaborators and interlocutors who ensure its eventual place in the public realm; nothing, in fact, could be further from Fried's Kantian defense of the autonomy of the artwork. Becker acknowledges his own potential bias against the specialness of the artist, as he was coming from a non-aesthetic background; the nature of his arguments also supports the conclusion that he was depending on a Marxist interpretation of art as production.\* The book suffers somewhat from trying to create a unified study of all the arts; the difficulty of covering them all prevents him from arriving at a close analysis of any one of the fields.† Similarly, by virtue of its emphasis on the division of labor in art, the essay, Becker also acknowledged, "does not attempt to develop a sociologically based theory of aesthetics" and it doesn't try to go far beyond more or less endorsing a general institutional theory of art criticism (subsequent debates around contemporary art and taste in the field were framed, rather, by Pierre Bourdieu's *La Distinction* of 1979, which establishes a stronger relationship between the construction of taste and class). Finally, as a book published three decades ago, *Art Worlds* can't provide us with sufficient tools to understand the many fluctuations that have occurred in contemporary art—most importantly, the effects that globalization has had on artmaking, the emergence of that international market of biennials and art fairs, the "emancipation" of the viewer through social media, and the increasing ability of artists to appropriate institutional contexts and create incursions into other areas of human activity (the various "turns": ethnographic, educational, etc.) in the creation of their work.

---

\* In his *Economic and Philosophic Manuscripts of 1844*, Marx discusses the role of labor in the development of man's capacity to perceive and reproduce the beautiful and to form objects also "in accordance with the laws of beauty." Karl Marx and Friedrich Engels, *Collected Works*, Vol. 3 (Moscow: International Publishers, 1975), p. 277.
† Although, it should be said, this is true of other sociological works that refer to "the art world" in an ambiguously expansive way, such as those of George Dickey and Arthur Danto's *The Artworld*.

However, Becker's main contribution may be the introduction of symbolic interactionism—a sociological theory that originated with George Herbert Mead and Charles Horton Cooley—as a tool to read the art world. In this Becker is also indebted to Chicago sociologist Herbert Blumer, who characterizes human behavior in relation to objects in the following ways: "Humans act toward things on the basis of the meanings they ascribe to those things"; "The meaning of such things is derived from, or arises out of, the social interaction that one has with others and the society"; and "These meanings are handled in, and modified through, an interpretative process used by the person in dealing with the things he encounters."* Becker describes a more nuanced social topography in art-making: he speaks about artists, producers, and critics, many of whom are "well-socialized members" of a particular art community, and the role of the public itself, arguing that the art world (or art worlds, in his case) is a constantly changing environment with a large group of agents that contribute in many ways to give meaning to every kind of art. Symbolic interactionism is, I believe, still a helpful way to conduct a reading of how values are socially constructed in art.

Before proceeding to discuss specific social scripts of art, it is important to clarify why we should consider our actions in society as performance and why such performance is an interpretive act. Our role as actors in the art world is connected to Fried's idea that self-consciousness inevitably leads to theatricality. It would be hard not to

---

\* Herbert Blumer, *Symbolic Interactionism: Perspective and Method*, (Berkeley: University of California Press, 1969), p. 2.

concede that the problem of authenticity extends not just to art-making but also to our social interactions in general, given that we can see ourselves in the art world, and it is difficult to extricate ourselves from our own self-perception. Conveying an "authentic" persona can be extremely difficult when we are dominated by self-consciousness.

For that reason, as artists, perhaps the greatest challenge is to perform, in our behavior, an accurate interpretation of what we deem an authentic version of ourselves, and in such a way that we may satisfactorily conclude that it is being interpreted correctly by others in the art world.

And the knowledge that we need to be true to ourselves, but that the best way to be truthful is through the use of somewhat artificial means (as the epigraph by Julio Torri suggests), forces all of us, to an extent, to be actors in the art world.

In the philosophy of culture, there are a number of thinkers, such as Erving Goffman and Clifford Geertz, who employ dramaturgical metaphors or parameters to understand social behavior. Within this tradition, and more recently, philosopher David Velleman has argued that the way we interact with each other in society resembles the actions of improvisational actors.* Moreover, he has argued that the construction of the self is a process that involves both fiction and truth: "We invent ourselves [. . .] but we really are the characters whom we invent."† This means that the roles we assume in a particular social envi-

---

\* David Velleman, *How We Get Along* (Cambridge: Cambridge University Press, 2009).
† Velleman, "The Self as Narrator," in John Philip Christman and Joel Anderson, eds., *Autonomy and the Challenges to Liberalism* (Cambridge: Cambridge University Press, 2005), p. 58.

ronment are not necessarily assigned to us, but rather are willingly adopted. In the process of making them our own, which is a process of searching for authenticity, we may fictionalize our true character and so become an authentic version of the fictional character we attempt to construct.

This perspective is particularly useful in examining the social dimension of the art world, because the environment of contemporary art, as previously described, is defined by a constant tension between a need for self-regulation and its historically contrarian spirit. In the long term, the binary relationship between the establishment (market and academia) and the laboratory (freewheeling creativity, experimentation, and the rebellion of art-making) functions rather as a well-oiled machine that quickly turns counterculture into mainstream culture and subsequently generates the impetus for new countercultural works. However, in daily and more routine reality, the establishment and the laboratory coexist awkwardly—when, for example, a museum trustee interacts with a radical young artist or when, as I will describe in chapter five, the director of an academic conference on art asks presenters to ensure that their presentations won't be conceived as performances.

To argue that performance is an interpretive act, we must briefly go over the meaning of "performance" and "interpretation" in the visual arts. In theater or music theory, performance is practically a synonym of interpretation, but in the visual arts the terms are used differently. Performance art, when it emerged as a term, described an experience delivered in an unmediated fashion, usually by the artist. In performance art, the work is not thought about in terms of how it was interpreted (unlike a theatrical piece or a violin performance): the person who in music is the interpreter is, in performance art, the originator of the work itself, and what's more, there are by definition no other possible interpreters of the piece (although this has changed recently; performance artists have started employing actors and creating "re-performances," a translation of performance art into theater).

Interpretation in the visual arts, as seen by hermeneutics (especially the thought of Hans-Georg Gadamer), is the interaction between a work and a viewer through the help of a "method" or mediating mechanism that supports the encounter—be it another person, a text, an audioguide, an app, etc. This process is enacted on a regular basis in museums and museum education departments, helping visitors get a sense of an artwork and assimilate or internalize it privately. To speak about the work, however, and do further actions in response to it (debating it with others, for example, or even making another artwork that stems from the viewing experience) is to engage in an interpretive performance of the kind that I described in music. When we externalize our response to the work (effectively translating it into an extrinsic value), our behavior is the result of our exposure to the many varieties of art and specific interpretations of art that we accept, are persuaded about, or adapt for ourselves, embodying the discourses that we are confronted with, through our own comments, actions, and conduct in general. Of course, if I am a person minimally aware of my surroundings and self-conscious about the possible repercussions of my comments, my acting may be conditioned by influential people around me, and I may follow their cues. The fact is that when one first enters the art world, it is no different than entering a party in the middle of the event. People are already in conversation groups, and a group dynamic has been set. As newcomers, our best option is to integrate ourselves into one of the groups and start following the tenor of the discussion, with the hope that we can at some point enter into the conversation. When we are in that situation, we are enacting an interpretive performance—we assess what is going on, follow cues as to what kind of comments are appropriate, and then enter, hoping to contribute in some way to what is being discussed. Any action that we make in relation to this world is a hermeneutic—that is, interpretive—response to group expectations: expectations relating to who we are in the field (artist, curator, student) and therefore what kind of input we can provide (whether we have firsthand experience of the subjects discussed, etc.). Because we are always somewhat unfamiliar with the parameters of the new world, a degree of interpretation and cue-following will always inform our acting. This is the way in which we become interpretive performers of the art world and the way we help construct an art scene.

Finally, there is yet another argument for the usefulness of understanding our current relationship with the art world as a stage on which we are required to perform; this one concerns nostalgia. In *Simulations*, Jean Baudrillard describes nostalgia thus:

When the real is no longer what it used to be, nostalgia assumes its full meaning. There is a proliferation of myths of origin and signs of reality; of second-hand truth, objectivity and authenticity. There is an escalation of the true, of the lived experience; a resurrection of the figurative where the object and substance have disappeared. And there is a panic-stricken production of the real and the referential, above and parallel to the panic of material production. This is how simulation appears in the phase that concerns us: a strategy of the real, neo-real and hyperreal, whose universal double is a strategy of deterrence.*

In the previous chapter I discussed how the recognition of familiar narratives plays a role in how we collectively construct value. For many years, the art world has suffered from an exhaustion of art narratives, which has led to a constant search for the next big development. In our spinning of these narratives (which I discuss further in chapter six of this book), we appear to be promoting things because they are new or transgressive, but in reality we are implicitly seeking validation through the recognition of the ways in which these new artists or artworks are the next rhyme in the poem of art history. In our peculiar art-world ways, we can't accept an exact imitation of the past, but we also can't accept something that is not in some kind of dialogue with the past; otherwise it would

---

* Jean Baudrillard, *Simulations*, From *Selected Writings*. (Stanford: Stanford University Press, 2002), p. 174.

appear incongruous. As a result, we act a new but somewhat nostalgic representation of the valued past, hoping that it will bring us again to that elusive combination of time and place that can become legendary. As in Greek mythology, we ultimately enact the familiar roles of culture: hero, antihero, enfant terrible, etc.

By far the greatest amount of communication about art occurs in an informal capacity, simply because formal education and formats of exchange occupy a small portion of our daily lives. Even in academic environments, where professionals are dedicated to the study of art, a substantial amount of the communication and discussion occurs outside the classroom or the lecture hall, in social events, gatherings, café discussions, and one-on-one conversations. In the art world, social gatherings are absolutely central to establishing consensus about a particular art or artist, exchanging information, conducting financial transactions, and positioning oneself favorably in the social network of art. This kind of professional networking is likely not different from that in other disciplines. The more complex aspect of the art world's social script is the way in which these exchanges influence taste, desirability, and consensus around the value of a particular artwork, artist, or group of artists. Events such as vernissages at art fairs and biennials are highly influential in directing trends in the market and high-level curatorial circles.

For those who are professionally involved in the art world, access to its inner circles is dependent on socializing and performing successfully in them. This entails that an actor agree to conform to a particular social role, as artist, curator, etc. These pre-established roles, and the specific demands on them, appear to be remarkably consistent throughout the world.* Some of their characteristics can be outlined as follows:

1. The consistency of behavior and social regulations in the established social environments of the art world is not usually something explicitly acknowledged or recognized, and it is learned informally through regular interaction within the art scene. While studio art programs have begun to offer professional skill development to introduce artists to the rudiments of promoting and selling their work, very little attention is given to how an artist should perform in specific professional scenarios and how to read and understand codes and cues from other professionals.
2. This lack of explicit acknowledgment of the social code within the art world often results in a great deal of anxiety for young professionals, who often fear being considered inadequate or appearing naïve or overly eager for attention.
3. Professional behavior in the contemporary art world requires restraint and at times even dishonesty (such as speaking favorably about an

---

* *The Pablo Helguera Manual of Contemporary Art Style*, one of my books (Tumbona, Mexico City, 2005) originally written in Spanish, has been translated into English, Hungarian, Croatian, and Korean, arguably because, according to the respective editors of each edition, the material presented is applicable to the local art worlds of these countries.

exhibition that one does not regard highly) in order not to endanger professional opportunities.
4. The non-academic script in the art world, applying the ideas of Pierre Bourdieu, is a class script based on exclusionary premises: the insider group thrives when a strong "cultivated disposition" is developed that distinguishes it from others.*

In summary, the art world today is broken into a myriad of art scenes, of tenuous networks that communicate through critical writing, commerce, social media, and mainly face-to-face events. Art continues to depend on that atmosphere of meaning to make sense, as Danto described. Art does not need to emerge from an art scene—"outsider" artists can and have been brought into the art world. However, if a work is to survive and play a role in the conversation of art, it must generate an art scene around it, a collectively constructed infrastructure such as the one described by Becker. The greatest difference between art made fifty years ago and the art of today is that all of us who inhabit the art world now have embodied (consciously or unconsciously) the realization that Warhol had at that opening in Philadelphia in 1965—*we* are the art; or, more accurately, the values and ideas of a particular work will inevitably be projected onto us, and we are crucial carriers of those ideas while being deeply self-conscious of the weight that such responsibility carries. We know that we are being scrutinized and observed,

---

* Pierre Bourdieu, *Distinction: A Social Critique on the Judgment of Taste* (Cambridge: Harvard University Press, 1984), p. 564.

and our actions respond to that awareness. We first act on the basis on how we understand the script, we modify or fine-tune our performance based on the reactions of others, and then, by taking in those reactions, we construct our values. And, like a role model who must project the values that he or she wants to impress upon others, we inevitably become the performers of the real-life character that we think we should be, or at least the one we want others to perceive.

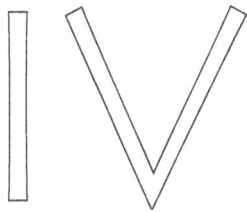

# THE DISRUPTIVE CHARACTER
## THE ARTISTIC SCRIPT

I often recall two conversations from a few years ago: one with a high-level New York museum curator, and another with a similarly influential Chelsea art gallery dealer. At a small internal meeting among museum staff, someone suggested that an exhibiting artist email acquaintances about a talk he was giving at the museum, in order to promote it; the curator quickly dismissed the notion, saying that it would be "inelegant" for the artist to directly promote his lecture. In my conversation with the dealer, we were talking about an artist who was asked by his gallery to personally deliver a recently purchased work of his to the collector. The dealer frowned at the idea, saying, "The reason there are galleries is because we help maintain a certain aura around the artist. Collectors like that aura. It may be just something symbolic, but it is important."

The point of these two incidental conversations is that both the dealer and the curator, accustomed to protecting the image of the artist in their own roles, intuitively concluded that any pedestrian contact between the artist and the public would somehow counter the uniqueness of the experience that is created by the mediated presentation of the work—and by extension, the image of the artist. No one denies that there is a certain level of artifice in the business of exhibiting art, and museums are specially designed to be temples that elevate objects above the level of the everyday—even when the art on view is precisely *about* the everyday. When the experience involves only the visitor and objects by the artist, the magic comes easily; but when the mortal self of the artist becomes involved things get confused; the "aura" threatens to dissipate.

The problem of maintaining an aura that guarantees the elevation of one's work to a realm of notoriety, while at the same time dealing with the terrestrial realities of everyday life, is very much on the mind of most artists. In his short novel *The Cloven Viscount* (1952), Italo Calvino narrates the story of a man who, while at war, becomes perfectly divided in two by a cannonball, but, miraculously, each of his two halves survives. One of them, which contains all the evil of his personality, goes around the world causing mischief; the other half, the good one, goes around doing good deeds—both of them end up being equally irritating to others. Eventually, after many tribulations, including a duel between the two, they are reattached by a doctor. Artists in today's art world have complicated divisions in their identities, as if divided by the cannonball of postmodernity, and a good deal of their efforts is focused on negotiating both halves.

An important problem in art history is the interpretation of an artist's biography in connection to his or her work. (In fact, it is no coincidence that the discipline of art history is considered to have been born with Giorgio Vasari's *Lives of the Artists*, in 1550.) In a discipline that gravitates toward narrative and storytelling, the artist's biography is a central source of information to the historian (and, in a different way, the critic) and can provide answers to a wide variety of questions regarding the artist's outlook on the world and his or her connections with other artists, influences, and personal biases.

The practice of biographical criticism in the visual arts was questioned in the 1920s by members of the New Criticism movement, who warned against what they called the "biographical fallacy"—that is, the tendency to read intentionality in artworks and relate their meaning to anecdotes from the life of the artist.* Beginning with the avant-garde and becoming more prevalent in the postwar era with the rise of performance art, interest grew among a number of artists in blurring the boundaries between their artwork and their lives. Marcel Duchamp, Salvador Dalí, Andy Warhol, and Martin Kippenberger are only a few artists who made their biographies nearly indistinguishable

---

\* See Donald J. Winslow, *Life Writing: A Glossary of Terms in Biography, Autobiography, and Related Forms*, 2nd ed. (Honolulu: University of Hawaii Press, 1995), p. 7.

from their artwork.* Their impulses included fabricating biographical data, obscuring some facts while highlighting others, and destroying early works and backdating others. Their gestures were a way to claim control over their own artistic narratives, which they knew would play a role in the analysis of their work.†

It is important to reflect on how the script of the artist's biography negotiates the relationship between the historical legacy of art history as biography and the ways artists participate in the fabrication of their own myths or images for history. Art history is a contested territory in which artists pass from being individuals, or subjects of culture, to being performers of culture, and the historian, as author of the academic script, imposes ownership on the narrative.

Artists are, at least nominally, the primary actors of the art scene. This much has remained true for most of the history of modern and contemporary art, although the definition of "artist" has experienced many changes and been the subject of debate. Today, the roles of artist, producer, and curator intermix in unprecedented ways. Star curators of major biennials get more play in the billing of the event than the artists themselves; the Solomon R. Guggenheim

---

* See Calvin Tompkins, *Marcel Duchamp: A Biography* (New York: Holt Paperback, 1998); Jessica Morgan, *Martin Kippenberger* (London: Tate, 2006); Andy Warhol, *The Philosophy of Andy Warhol* (Boston: Mariner Books, 1977); and Salvador Dalí, *The Secret Life of Salvador Dalí* (Whitefish, Mont.: Kessinger Publishing LLC, 2010).

† There are many examples of artists' consciousness of their own biographies. One is Andy Warhol's Time Capsule project. See "Andy Warhol: Time Capsules," The Warhol: Resources and Lessons, http://edu.warhol.org/app_aw_tc.html.

Museum, during the Thomas Krens era, featured a wide variety of artists, but the figure of Krens dominated them all; major art collectors demand their own starring roles in the museums they create or support. The protagonist role in art is a contested one, and today's artists struggle to keep their grip on it. Today it doesn't suffice to simply make art in the studio and send it out into the world: artists have to be active agents who advocate for their work, engage socially with those who may support them, and help shape the discourse in a way that will favor their artistic perspective. One may certainly, as an artist, ignore the social and economic dynamics of the art world and choose to produce work in isolation; this is a risky bet that most professional artists are not willing to make. Furthermore, to participate in the creation of an art scene is a great motivator for a creative type: one is challenged and influenced (in a healthy or unhealthy way) by the work of others, and can enact a similar influence, resulting in a stimulating experience for those involved in the conversation.

In the art world today, artists confront colossal competition for attention, not only among other artists, but also by equally ambitious or driven curators, collectors, museum directors, and even critics. The exchanges one enters with all these characters are, in small ways, negotiations for support. Like a theater actor, an artist is "cast" into a group exhibition that a "director" (the curator) has concocted. A poor exhibition may be attributed to a miscasting of the artists. In a similar fashion, renowned artists "adopt" go-to individuals (junior curators, writers, etc.) who may help support their careers.

Given the complex circumstances that an artist faces in his or her career, it is not enough, as previously mentioned, to simply remain in the studio and send the art into the world: an artist has to be an active actor in the art scene. This, in turn, presents yet another problem: the variety of actions, alliances, and behaviors that an artist may need to maintain in order to advance an art career may be at odds with the integrity of his or her work. A few truly eccentric artists may not understand this necessity, just as an outsider artist may be unsuspectingly adopted by the art world; they are, however, in the minority.

The previously mentioned work of sociologist Erving Goffman can help to explain the conundrum faced by the artist. Goffman's frame analysis theory revolves around the ways we define ourselves in relation to "frames" that we (or society) have constructed for ourselves. (Interestingly, Goffman uses the picture frame as a metaphor, as it effectively demarcates another reality.) When we contravene social conventions (for instance, if we misbehave at a party, becoming a rowdy guest), we are in an "out of frame" mode. "Out of frame" activity is unusual activity, often disruptive of the general harmony that frameworks contain.*

In the art world, which thrives on the expectation that the artist will cause some kind of disruption, we may have to invert the metaphor. In other words, an artist is behaving in the expected manner when he or she is behaving badly, fulfilling the role of the enfant terrible. In

---

\* Erving Goffman, *Frame Analysis: An Essay on the Organization of Experience* (Boston: Northeastern University Press, 1986).

mythological genealogy, if we recall the work of Lewis Hyde, the disruptive artist would be the trickster.*

The reality, however, is that the institutionalized structure of the art world today can only tolerate so much disruption from an artist. Christoph Büchel's canceled exhibition at Mass MoCA in 2007, and the subsequent debacle, is an interesting instance of what happens when an artist's demands become so unreasonable that they cause a breakdown in the support system (which is precisely what Büchel may have wanted to point out as part of his project).† Ultimately, an artist has to concede ground to the institution, whose limitations largely reflect the temporal, financial, and even legal frameworks of the art world. Artists are well aware of these limitations, and, as a result, whenever an artist with a reputation for transgressiveness enters into a collaboration with a museum, there is a very delicate negotiating process: both sides try to determine the point at which the exhibition will be viable as a public product and yet still respect the integrity of the artist and the work (a concern usually held as much by the museum as by the individual artist). In this instance, the frame (the museum institution) has been designed to allow the artist to behave disruptively.

When artists are pushed to make extreme concessions, or when they have to sacrifice the integrity of their work for reputational or commercial opportunities, they are thrown into "out of frame" territory. In those instances,

---

* Lewis Hyde: *Trickster Makes This World*. (London: Macmillan, 2010.)
† For more information about this unrealized exhibition, see *The Mass MoCA Blog*, http://blog.massmoca.org/category/training-ground/.

artists have to develop "out of frame" public personae that are nonetheless consistent with the message that their "in frame" work is perceived to have. For example, think of artists who produce work that is admired for the way it challenges the establishment; they are often severely attacked when it is perceived that they have "sold out" to commercial success. A prominent example is Marina Abramović. Abramović's performance art from the 1970s, like much of the work produced at that time, had little or no commercial objective; in fact, it was made to challenge the art market. As her work became known, it also became appropriated by others, ranging from artists to even the commercial mainstream. Over the last decade, Abramović started to show a concern for her legacy, publicly declaring her intention to reclaim her work; this led to something close to the trademarking of her work as belonging to the "Abramović Method." The trademarking process retroactively commodified the earlier performance work—the very artworks whose materiality, at that time it was made, performance artists were deliberately challenging. I don't intend to judge Abramović for this decision—many would agree that artists don't have to follow the same ideas for their entire careers, and many also understand the logic behind this change, although the perception that this change of rules does a disservice to the original ideas behind performance art is also entirely valid. But the larger point is that the changing of strategy—in this case, ironically, by a performance artist—represents a rewriting of roles by the artist that negotiates the historical arc of her work, offering a logic that, in her view, respects the integrity of her career. The conundrum faced by a performance artist like Abramović is not faced so much by artists whose work has always been part of the art market—say, Jasper Johns. This is not to say that artists whose work is more conventionally linked to the art market don't face hard questions about their actions, particularly when their work appears to veer into opportunism or sacrifice criticality from commercial expediency.

In addition to this challenge, which we may define as the search for authenticity, artists have to engage in an art system that requires a certain stability in order to properly perform its function as a support to their art-making. This necessity enters into conflict with the yearning for freedom and experimentation that is common to all contemporary art. This tension is obviously not new: modern art was born out of the rebellion of the *refusé* artists against the standards and program of the Academy. The story of twentieth-century art is what Octavio Paz once described as a "tradition of rupture," the notion that a new generation of artists will inevitably challenge the status quo created by the previous generation and, through that very challenge, ironically uphold a tradition of rejecting the immediate past while acknowledging its influence on the present.*

This constant need to destabilize or break the scheme without entirely renouncing it has been one of the greatest challenges for artists since the 1960s, especially when the anti-institutionalist thinking of that period started permeating a good deal of art production, leading to

---

* Octavio Paz, *Children of the Mire: Modern Poetry from Romanticism to the Avant-Garde.* (Boston: Harvard University Press, 1991), p. vi.

process-based art, identity politics, and institutional critique. Artists—and, as a result, most other art world professionals—had to construct a new role for themselves. The parasite, irritant, or trickster seemed the right role to continue to assume, continuing the modernist tradition. But artists increasingly needed to play an "out of frame" role also; a somewhat functional persona that would allow the dysfunctional one to exist. This functional, "out of frame" persona is the pragmatist, the one with the longer career view, the one who attends dinners with collectors and other supporters—the negotiator with the "behind the scenes", as it were, of the art world. This second self, necessarily more conventional, is usually seen only in private among a few insiders or people in the inner circle of the artist. The second self is a regulator/mediator between the artist's first persona and the world.

Many artists are very uncomfortable with the construction of this second self, which to an extent negates the purity of the public "radical" artist persona. Part of the importance of Andy Warhol lies in his open embrace of commerce as part of his identity, which allowed other artists, such as Jeff Koons and Damien Hirst, to follow a similar line. But as is particularly exemplified in Hirst's case, it continues to be difficult for an artist to openly commercialize his or her work without risking negative regard by critical circles in the art world. And in those instances where an artist publicly renounces the art market or the established system of exhibition, in museums, biennials, or galleries, he or she may still maintain a dialogue with it through academia, publications, and social events.

In practice then, artists tend to perform not just one or two, but sometimes a multiplicity of selves, all of which are interconnected but distinct in their purpose, but the primary relationship is between the public and the private persona.

As I will describe in the next section, this script interlocks with—and in fact, becomes subsumed by—another script, one that doesn't suffer from the public vs. private conundrum but that instead is challenged by the relationship between text and spoken word: the academic script.

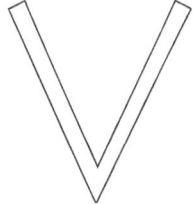

# THE REGULATING CHARACTER
## THE ACADEMIC SCRIPT

In September 2010, the director of programs of the College Art Association (CAA) in New York sent a letter to all the session chairs for its upcoming annual conference—the gathering with the highest profile among university art programs in the United States and the highest attendance from their members. The letter read as follows:

> Dear Session Chair,
>
> At a recent CAA conference a session participant assumed the identity of a living scholar and made a presentation in that guise. This impersonation was part of a performance event that was not made known to CAA or to the person whose identity was stolen. This dishonest action in the guise of art was

deeply troubling and embarrassing for the victim and for CAA.

I am writing to ask you to verify that the information presented to you by speakers is original, that the participants in your session are who they claim to be, and that your session is not a performance, unless it has been presented as such in your application to the program committee.*

The CAA conference has long been the premier event at which universities interview and recruit new professors for their arts programs and promote their publications and at which art historians deliver their papers and research. At the same time, the conference's presentation format has been criticized as too tedious, as audiences usually end up sitting for hours listening to academics reading papers on a variety of specialized subjects. The spoken public presentation is central in the field of visual arts, particularly in the area of adult learning. In addition to academic conferences, public program departments in museums present lectures or discussions about art involving artists, art historians, and theorists. Yet, very little qualitative analysis has been conducted on the effectiveness of these presentations. Often, public presentations are deemed impenetrable, obscure, or ineffective†—what can be communicated in writing cannot always be easily grasped when presented on stage. Program

---

\* Letter by Emmanuel Lemakis, Director of Programs, College Art Association, to the session leaders, September 16, 2010.
† See Tariq Tahir, "Are You Reaching Those at the Back?," *The Times Higher Education*, January 10, 2008, http://www.timeshighereducation.co.uk/story.asp?storyCode=400073&sectioncode=26.

participants usually have no way of comparing their level of comprehension to that of others. A critical evaluation does not typically follow this type of public presentation, and so it is difficult to fully understand what determines a presentation's effectiveness or failure.*

Because of the general exasperation with the shortcomings of the academic presentation, every now and then a panel discussion is organized at an academic conference that tries to infuse new energy through experimental or guerrilla tactics. Such was the incident the CAA letter referred to, which took place at the conference in 2010. The gesture brought together two parts of the art world that coexist with great difficulty: on the one hand, the rebellious, anti-establishment artistic impulse that characterizes most of the history of the visual arts and, on the other hand, the order-seeking world of academia, which aims to document, study, organize, narrate, and analyze art movements from a detached and hopefully objective distance. The tension between these two elements generates situations such as that faced by the CAA's director of programs, in which conference representatives find themselves attempting to eradicate non-approved art from the confines of a conference about art. The tenor of this tension is also precisely what propels some of the most entertaining action of the art world—the ways in which the performative impulse manifests itself in formal and informal exchanges around art. I have previously

---

* I explored this subject in *Art Speech—A Symposium on Symposia*, a conference I organized and codirected with historian James Elkins at the Museum of Modern Art, New York, May 20, 2011.

described the artistic script as the "disruptive," mostly informal script. Its regulating, stabilizing counterpart is the academic script.*

Academic writing in the visual arts largely follows the same standards as other branches of the humanities. The three primary areas of academic activity in the visual arts are the theory of studio art instruction (which is different from the pragmatics of teaching art in the studio), art history, and art theory. These three areas of self-reflexivity in the visual arts have been present since the emergence, during the Renaissance, of the modern concept of art.† In other words, the need to instruct on forms of art-making, chronicle those forms and tendencies, and theorize about the meaning of these forms can be regarded as natural extensions of art practice itself. At the same time, however, the articulation of the artistic experience in words has always kept the writer at a certain distance from the subject, for a number of reasons. The most evident is the fact that any interpretation of the visual in writing is an imperfect proposition, as images can't objectively be translated into words. The less evident reason, which has been studied by art historians including James Elkins, is that the demands of philosophical, historical, and pedagogical discourse on concrete artworks are such that resulting texts are only

---

* By "academic script" (in the visual arts) I refer not to written and published scholarship on contemporary art but rather to the way in which this activity (the activity of research, writing, publishing, etc.) influences social and professional behavior.
† See Hans Belting, *Likeness and Presence: History of the Image before the Era of Art* (Chicago: University of Chicago Press, 1997).

partial interpretations or representations of those artworks, yet they are often assigned a kind of objectivity.*

## Subscripts: academic as arbiter, academic as narrator

The CAA letter exemplifies the academic role of the reactive regulator, or arbiter, of the artist—attempting to impose some order and critical frame onto the overflowing energy of the art experience. The complementary subscript, as it were, is the one in which the academic adopts a more active stance, by becoming the "storyteller" of a particular art historical period or the interpretive voice that lays out a particular subject.

The distance between theory and praxis in the visual arts is best understood in the textual analysis of art, because it is through the practice of writing that scholarship is taught and developed. Art history and philosophy of art programs seldom include art-making as a requirement, but, more importantly, the performative component of pedagogy receives very little attention. This means that academics, when communicating their (mostly written) ideas to an audience, usually conform to very traditional methods of academic presentation (the twenty-page paper, for example, or the slide lecture). Usually involving reading from notes in set patterns of monotonous intonation, this verbal delivery has as its implicit aim to be as neutral as possible by virtue of its purely nondescript qualities.

In order to understand the common challenges of what I term "visual arts speech," it is useful to refer to John L.

---

\* See James Elkins, *Our Beautiful, Dry, and Distant Texts: Art History as Writing* (Philadelphia: The Pennsylvania State University Press, 1997).

Austin's theory of speech acts, and work by Donald A. Bligh on lecturing. According to Austin, speech acts can be analyzed on three levels: locutionary (ostensible meaning), illocutionary (intended meaning), and perlocutionary (actual effect).* Using this rubric, one can argue that the locutionary and illocutionary aspects of a visual arts speech are separated from its perlocutionary aspect. Examples of this fact abound. For example, I recently conducted a public experiment with a class of art educators in Porto Alegre, Brazil. I started my lecture by reading aloud a written description of the painting *Las Meninas*, by Diego Velázquez.† In this short paragraph I included a standard grouping of data, quotes, and interpretive and objective information about the painting, similar to an encyclopedia entry. Immediately after reading it I asked the audience of three hundred attendees to repeat, with the closest accuracy possible, what I had just said. Out of that audience not a single participant was able to recall the paragraph word by word; only a handful of listeners were able to approximate close to seventy-five percent of what I had said through paraphrasing, and a much larger amount of listeners were able to recall a handful of words and data.

That experiment brings me to Bligh's book *What's the Use of Lectures*, first published in 1971.‡ In that work Bligh

---

* John L. Austin, *How to Do Things with Words* (Cambridge, Mass.: Harvard University Press, 1962).
† Inaugural lecture by the author to participants of the annual course for art educators at the Mercosul Biennial, Porto Alegre, Brazil, May 25, 2011.
‡ Donald Bligh, *What's the Use of Lectures*. (San Francisco, CA: Jossey-Bass, 2000).

argues that the format of the lecture is not more effective, and is indeed sometimes less effective, than other modes of communication in persuading listeners or communicating a given set of ideas. Bligh's work is consistent with most of the pedagogical thinking of the twentieth century around the importance of the use of dialectics in teaching. Through a number of studies, Bligh shows that the lack of participation and involvement of the audience while listening to a lecture takes them into a near-dormant state, in which attentiveness to what is being said decreases.

**FIGURE 17.1. MEAN HEART RATES DURING TWO TEACHING PERIODS.**

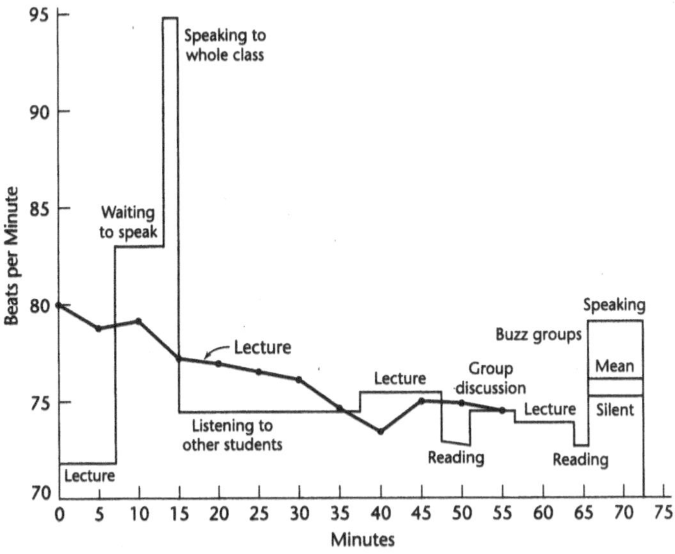

Graph from *What's the Use of Lectures?*, by Donald Bligh (p. 255), showing levels of student stimulation during a lecture. See ‡ note on p. 58.

Art history definitely has performative heroes. One of the recurring personalities in this regard is Kirk Varnedoe (1946–2003), a legendary curator at the Museum of Modern Art, New York, characterized by his eloquence and highly articulate speech. A close examination of videos of Varnedoe's public lectures reveals a charismatic, good-looking individual with a slight southern accent (Varnedoe was from Georgia) who speaks, as a colleague of mine once remarked, "in full paragraphs," without notes and with complete self-assurance and ease. Few curators or art historians are so adaptable to performing their role on camera as Varnedoe was. He rarely, if ever, spoke from a prepared text—that is, he did not adhere to a pre-established script, instead fluctuating seamlessly between an "in frame" and "out of frame" persona (if such a distinction may be made in his case). Leo Steinberg (1920–2011) is a similar case, an inspirational figure for generations of art historians who was famous for his eloquence. Robert Rosenblum (1927–2006), with whom I had the opportunity to work, was famous among his students at the Institute of Fine Arts at New York University for a game in which students would randomly place slides showing artworks into a carrousel (when slide projectors were still being used in schools), based on which he would spontaneously deliver a coherent lecture. T.J. Clark, who has had a wide-ranging influence on generations of younger historians, is known for his erudite analysis expressed with literary sophistication, often honoring his own comment, "Lyric cannot be expunged from modernism, only repressed."*

Exceptions like these, however, only confirm the larger gravitational force of academia, which pulls the speaker toward homogeneity of tone, to reading from notes, and to rarely detaching from conventions. There is a vast difference between these stars of art history and the average, introspective academic delivering his or her dry paper at an art history conference. Aside from the value of the content of their texts, the main contrast between the experienced and conventional academic performer is in their delivery.

Traditional academic presentations in the visual arts, by virtue of being speech acts as well as acts of pedagogical persuasion, are usually ineffective in two ways: first, because their basis in language limits their ability to properly "translate" the art experience into words, and second, because, in their live form, they are ineffective communicators of an original or intended meaning to an audience. Given this, it remains to ask why art historians are not better trained as lecturers and why the art history profession is generally content with traditional modes of delivery.

An immediate answer is that, for the main purposes of academia, the construction of a compelling public persona, while desirable, is not critical. The performer can be impersonal as long as the information provided in the

---

* Timothy J. Clark, *Farewell to an Idea: Episodes from a History of Modernism* (New Haven, Conn.: Yale University Press, 2001), p. 401. Ellen Levy explored Clark's relationship with poetry in her lecture "The Deep Ludicrousness of Lyric: The Poet in T.J. Clark," at The School of Visual Arts, New York, April 12, 2011.

paper is considered sound. The academic script, in other words, allows for the enacting of a neutral character that is closer to the printed essay.

In contrast to the artistic script, in which the artist negotiates between his or her public persona and the behavior of a more conventional second self, the academic script has to both achieve the translation of the visual act into something verbal—that is, becoming a successful "narrator" of art—and successfully bridge the illocutionary and perlocutionary acts. To do this, those in the business of chronicling and interpreting the visual arts (critics, academics, curators) resort to a variety of strategies to create their interpretive performances.

This interpretive performance of the visual within the narrative/academic realm must strive for objectivity and be informed, but, perhaps most important, it also needs to *sound* persuasive. It may seem strange to say that it is more important for a successful performance to *appear* meaningful than *be* meaningful, but that is really the difference between the illocutionary and perlocutionary aspects of speech.

This gap exists for two reasons: the first has to do with the audience, and the second has to do with the speaker. As demonstrated in my experiment with *Las Meninas*, the spectator/audience member can't possibly grasp absolutely every word and gesture the speaker expresses; perception is full of distractions, including the listener's own thoughts as he or she listens, and the memory only retains a small portion of what was said.*

Another factor that affects the reception of academic speech is the level of expertise that the speaker may (or may not) have in the subject being discussed and his or her talent at communicating it to the audience, as well as the previous knowledge that the audience member may have on the subject. For example, if I am not a specialist in, say, Arte Povera, and I attend an Arte Povera gallery talk by a curator in a museum, how can I know if the curator knows the material? And if I am the curator, how can I successfully bridge what I mean to say with the actual effect of what I am saying?

The speaker may attempt to communicate a particular message to an audience, but depending on the delivery it may not have the desired effect (it may be confusing, sound contradictory, etc.). If a speaker develops skills to understand the perlocutionary effect of a particular verbal or physical gesture, then he or she will become a good communicator. Studying the demeanor of the eminences of art history (Varnedoe, Clark, etc.) as captured on video, we can identify a variety of gestures and modalities of speech that, if they differ substantially in substance or content, are very similar in form—the assuredness in tone, the omnipresent, narrative voice that we instinctively associate

---

* According to educator Edgar Dale, we retain ten percent of what we read, twenty percent of what we hear, fifty percent of what we see and hear, seventy percent of what we talk about with others, eighty percent of what we experience, and ninety-five percent of what we "do" as a performed task. E. Dale, *Audiovisual Methods in Teaching* (New York: Dryden Press, 1969).

with authority, and the vast vocabulary and repertoire of phrases that present a straightforward fact in a lyrical form, creating a greater impact on the listener.

As members of the audience, informed professionals, when they try to ascertain the validity of a presentation on a subject they don't have full familiarity with or full command of the facts about, will look for the qualities of objectivity and knowledge in the speaker; but for those (the large majority) who don't actively participate in shaping the debate on taste and valuation in the visual arts or keep up with the language and codes particular to discussions of contemporary art, appreciation of a knowledgeable curator ends up being more textural and less based on the evaluation of concrete statements; that is, it depends on the recognition of forms that convey assurance, authority, and nuance of discourse. Listening to a great speaker, even if we don't understand a word he or she is saying, we can recognize aspects of his or her speech that we normally associate with wisdom and knowledge, such as the frequency and depth of cultural references, the contrasting of various historical and aesthetic ideas, the sophistication of the articulation of the arguments, and so forth. Similarly, this persona usually includes the projection of connoisseurship and authority, and the confidence that such qualities inspire. In the case of the Arte Povera gallery talk, I may not be able to ascertain the validity of the claims the curator is making, but I can get a sense of the level of detail in which she is discussing the works and the degree to which she is tying the works and artists with historical moments. I can compare (intuitively perhaps) the way she is speaking about the objects to the way in which I have seen authorities speak on other topics. Based on those perceptions, I might make a provisional assessment that the curator knows what she is talking about and that I should trust her comments.

This is the great opening that allows the mediocre scholar, curator, or writer to offer a lecture that will be perceived as an informed assessment of a subject, utilizing the sophisticated rhetorical turns that we often associate with an informed opinion, when in reality it is nothing more than a simulation of the transmission of knowledge. In such a case, the interpretive performer relies heavily on the histrionics of authority—that is, on those familiar patterns that we are generally conditioned to perceive as belonging to someone who knows what they are talking about. This phenomenon was unveiled in 1970 through an experiment by three psychology professors. They presented an actor as "Doctor Myron L. Fox," an "authority on the application of mathematics on human behavior," and had him deliver a lecture with charisma and authority, yet without any coherent content or substance. The unsuspecting student attendees, queried on the quality of the lecture, consistently remarked that they were satisfied with the presentation and had found it interesting overall. The study concluded that the students' satisfaction with learning was based mainly on the illusion of having learned.*

Here it is also important to point out that just as

---

\* Donald H. Naftulin, M.D., John E. Ware, Jr., and Frank A. Donnelly, "The Doctor Fox Lecture: A Paradigm of Educational Seduction," *Journal of Medical Education*, vol. 48, July 1973: 630–35.

there is a vast gradation of ability among speakers and performers, there are also more than just expert and inexpert listeners. In between, for example, there could be a sophisticated audience member who isn't knowledgeable about the subject at hand but who is familiar with lectures and with art in general, and who, using that experience, could get a good sense of whether the performance and remarks of the speaker add up to a meaningful whole.

When the performer is unable to appropriately convey authority, or to persuade others of the value of a particular artist or idea, the performance of the academic interpreter is deemed to have failed. The anxiety associated with the academic script in the visual arts leads performers to revert to the comfort zone of the local academic rhetoric: an over-dependence on the PowerPoint presentation, the excessive deference to other voices (either of authoritative art historians or the artists themselves), the enumeration of historical facts, and also a particular monotonousness of voice, imitating familiar patterns of melodic voice that we normally associate with the impersonal, instructional academic tone.

This intentionally restricted range of live presentation formats in the academic realm, as I mentioned at the beginning of the chapter, enters by design into tension with the artistic script. The scripts often merge like this: the academic establishes a theoretical or interpretive framework, the artist enters to disrupt this framework or create paradoxes that question it, the academic comes back to document what the artist has done, interpret it and propose a new framework, and so forth, ad infinitum.

The appropriation of academic language by artists with an ironic stance is best exemplified by the artworks grouped under institutional critique—starting from Robert Morris's 1963 lecture performance entitled *21.3* in which he had an actor lip synch a recorded lecture by Erwin Panofsky, and exemplified by Andrea Fraser's channeling of the docent Jane Castleton in *Museum Highlights*, in 1989. In instances like those, artists impersonate the academic to enact a critique of academicism. In reality, both Morris (via a hired actor, which adds even more layers) and Fraser were interpreting the character that the academic often also interprets—they were commenting on the "in frame" character of the academic. In these and similar works, the academic is a readymade object signifying rigidity of thinking, conservatism, and, ultimately, the establishment. (It would be most innovative, I would dare to suggest, for the academic to one day impersonate the artist, for art history programs to make students act as the artists they are studying.*)

The paradox of this dynamic is that, as time passes, and as new artworks become subject to interpretation, historicization, and theorization, the parameters for "in frame" scripts shift. For example, if an artist were to repeat an action or artwork that was considered too radical thirty or forty years ago, it is not likely that the work would be considered radical today.

This pattern, however is disrupted by new ideas and actions that point to where the new fourth wall—the

---

* An example of this attempt to merge or confuse roles between artist and academic is the Chicago-based collective "Our Literal Speed."

edge of the frame—lies at that particular moment. It is the edge of the dream, where, as Novalis says, we can finally separate ourselves from the reality we experience and acquire perspective on it.

This also means that in the art world, when the actors play their roles (instead of breaking them), the debate tends to become, overall, an academic one. Conceptual art, political art, performance art, and activist art are all subject to academization, and while they may retain an aspect of radicality, they are mostly "in frame" forms that are easily contained within the academic script. Because of this, the academic script has become the dominant script in the art scene, as the majority of characters take its cues, tending toward standardization.

Therein lies one of the greatest ironies of the universe of art scenes: despite the fact that the art world praises itself as a sphere of innovation and progressive thinking, most of the time its actors perform nostalgic derivations of derivative performances, which are deemed to be new or pattern-altering, making something that is considered to be radical when, in fact, it is fairly predictable. This is because we, as performative interpreters, contribute to a retrofeeding world of simulations of simulations, in which the original idea or point of the interpretation has receded deeply into the background. This is evident most clearly in the fact that there is such a narrow variety in the art world's social rituals, conventions, and other, similar exchanges. This retrofeeding of simulations may also explain why it has become so hard to parody certain individuals whose antics and personalities have become inextricable from the art scene: they are, in themselves, already parodies, to the point that we have become inoculated to even the most ironic representations of them. This kind of contrived acting for ourselves may be an inevitable adjustment but may be also an indicator of blind solipsism within the society of art, leading to the death of irony.

It is perplexing to think that, in the same way that audience members can be falsely convinced that they have learned something at a spurious lecture, active and even knowledgeable participants of the art scene can easily become—and I believe constantly do become—deluded by simulations of innovation. In the art world, a dramaturgical force actively seeks to create the suspension of disbelief. In its interaction with its counterpoint, the discourse, it constitutes the larger narrative arch of the art scene.

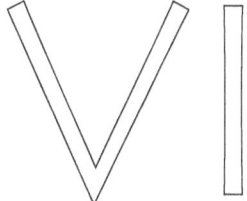

# Distribution, Discourse, and Subsidiary Scripts

Konjit Seyoum, an Ethiopian artist, started exhibiting her work in Addis Ababa in 1996—a time when, in that city, there were no art galleries. She resorted to exhibiting her work at her own home. She organized an opening of sorts and prepared a lot of food to entice people to attend, and it worked. Eventually, people got used to coming to her house to view her exhibitions. Before long, she had competition: other people followed her example and also started throwing parties at their homes, featuring art exhibitions of their own.

She was, however, not entirely satisfied: she wanted critical reception for her work. Because there were no art critics, she took upon it herself, writing a self-critique of her work that she later distributed. As with the home exhibitions and parties, others also followed suit.* Thus, slowly, by her own accord, and single-handedly, she did two things: she created a mode of distribution for her work, and she created a conversation about it. She created an art scene.

The circumstances of Seyoum's story are drastically different from those of internationally interconnected art scenes—the semiprivate spheres of biennials, art fairs, and galleries—but it nonetheless contains elements that accurately relate to behavior around taste and value on a larger scale.

In economic terms, Seyoum intuitively produced a theater of consumption—an environment that advertised a specific good (her own artwork) through a series of social enticements—a welcoming space, with food, in which people could enjoy themselves while also experiencing her work. The significance of this fact is twofold: on the one hand, she presented Ethiopian society with a paradigm for which there were no recognizable precedents; nor did it replace any previous paradigms (as we are forced to do in heavily populated and history-charged urban centers). Simultaneously, on the other hand, she introduced a paradigm that out of necessity conflated elements normally kept separate: someone makes the art, another person curates the show, sometimes another person promotes the exhibition, another writes a review. As in a Kabuki play, Seyoum managed to do all of it, and no one seemed to object, as there was no previous model to compare it to.

---

* Konjit Seyoum, in conversation with the author, at Apexart, New York, 2003.

Technically, she was playing all the roles of the art scene: the artistic and the academic characters, all within the forces of discourse and distribution.

I had a related experience of a city that largely exists outside the art world network—in 2006, when I visited Asunción, Paraguay, to present an art project. It was immediately apparent that the project was automatically relevant for the local community by the mere fact that it was taking place. A local artist told me: "You are the first foreign artist to come to Asunción in ten years." Whether this was true or not, the statement accurately reflected the collective feeling that having an international art project visiting the town was in itself meaningful enough to stir excitement and conversation. This experience contrasted with my visit, days later, to Buenos Aires to present the same project. In that city, where there is a sophisticated and highly articulated art scene, it most definitely was not enough to simply arrive and present the project, as, in that city, having foreign artists visit is not a notable occurrence. Instead, the project was highly scrutinized and subject to discussion, so much so that the discussion ultimately eclipsed the content of the artwork. In that instance, I was presented with the much more complex task of inserting the project into the discourse of the local art scene, which required me to very carefully consider the words I used to describe it.*

---

* For more information about this exchange, see Adetty Perez de Miles, "Revolution/Institution, Public Art, and Answerability: The Transnational Dialogic Encounters of The School of Panamerican Unrest," in *The School of Panamerican Unrest: An Anthology of Documents*, Pablo Helguera and Sara Demeuse, eds. (New York: Jorge Pinto Books, 2011), p. 61.

While it may be hard for someone accustomed to the art world in New York or London to conceive of a one-person art scene, I believe that the examples of Seyoum and Asunción/Buenos Aires, from their microscopic scale, can help us understand the complex dynamics of construction of value that result in the larger theater of consumption of the art world, and the complex relationships that today exist among advertising, market visibility, critical reception, and the long-term impact of a work.

The two examples outlined above are meant to illustrate the argument that the existing local discourse and the social context (or lack thereof) of an art scene are key to the reception of an art project. Artists do not exist in a vacuum: in order for us to be actors in the art scene, we need to be part of the action (the discourse) and do it in a visible way (distribution). Whenever one of these is not present, we need to create it ourselves; and whenever it exists, we need to insert ourselves in it.

To explain the influence of distribution and discourse in the social scripts of the art world, we must first understand the relationship of the art scene to posterity. Art-making and the series of exchanges that surround it—social, verbal, monetary—are generally enacted with the expectation that they will have a long-term impact. This means that just as artists hope to influence the field in an enduring way (or at least be more than a passing fad), contemporary art collectors want the work they invest in to rise in value and prominence, affirming their foresight in collecting it in the first place. (I imagine there are collectors who intentionally acquire work that they know will be considered worthless in the future, but most would agree that this is not the norm.)

As actors in the art scene we are very connected to the present, but we also hope that what we are doing is meaningful, and to be meaningful is to endure beyond the present moment. The challenge of being an art producer is to ultimately contribute to the larger narrative of art. Given this fact, and because the environment is saturated by those who are competing with each other to make their statements, we are generally forced—either personally or through promoters and supporters of our work—to enter into the game of distribution: the way by which our work becomes known and, by virtue of being known, becomes influential.

The process of taste construction in contemporary art is not only inextricable from, but actually dependent on, the impact of its promotion. Yet it is common wisdom that promotion and distribution alone don't necessarily improve the collective perception of an artwork and that they most certainly don't guarantee, in any case, its passing "the test of time." As proof of this perception, in three-decades-old issues of art magazines we encounter numerous ads and articles about artists who today we know little or nothing about, while only a handful of those referenced in the issue remain recognized. However, publicity and value formation are linked in deeper ways, in which artworks/artists can acquire a relevance that can affect their value.

Here I need to explain what I mean by *a relevance that can affect their value*. Whenever we speak about an artwork/artist having a meaningful or consequential impact in an art scene, certain events need to have happened beforehand for it to have had *any* impact whatsoever: it is dependent on how the artwork/artist has performed in the art realm up to that moment, and how the members of the art scene have performed in relation to it (that is, how the works have inserted themselves in public arenas of discussion, such as social events, publications, and the like).

Distribution is a form of ensuring visibility in the same way that content is a form of promoting collective consensus, or critical mass. I briefly elaborate on both of these below.

### DISTRIBUTION AS VISIBILITY

In the overcharged art world of today, with the extensive proliferation of art centers and intense art production everywhere, great artworks only become meaningful when they become visible in the professional art media (including online and offline art magazines, academic publications, etc.). There are, of course, artists who produce work in isolation. But if the work is to become part of the discourse, it must be brought into it by someone at some point. This was the case with Henry Darger, the eccentric outsider artist who worked in isolation and secrecy all of his life. His work was discovered by his landlords, Nathan and Kiyoko Lerner, who took it upon themselves to promote it. Today Darger's work is firmly ensconced in contemporary art collections and is increasingly influential among artists.

But it is not enough, of course, to be visible: the conditions in which this visibility takes place carry an enormous degree of significance in the art world. There are universally recognizable ways in which visibility creates value in an artist—when an artist exhibits at a major, reputable institution, for example. But there are other forms of visibility, which may be more subtle but are recognized by many as meaningful—such as when an influential collector or groups of collectors start investing in the work of a particular artist.

It can be argued that, under this logic, the art market should dominate the theater of the consumption of art, since it is fueled by the institutions that can make works most visible. However, while works that become ubiquitous do have an impact in the art world (negative or positive), the art world doesn't evaluate art on the sole basis of how famous or recognizable it is; aside from being visible, the work needs to instigate conversation and reflection. It needs to insert itself into the discourse, which brings me to the next factor.

## Discourse as Critical Mass

Following the extensive distribution or dissemination of a particular work or idea, individuals may become adopters of it or converts to it, and help it become part of the discourse. In social dynamics, the process of adoption doesn't require that the event, work, or idea be positive or good—social stigmas, for instance, also are adopted by many and reach their own "critical mass."

This is another way to say that even though art can't become meaningful until it has been inserted into the discourse of the art scene, becoming meaningful doesn't necessarily require that it expresses deep and provocative ideas or offers a strong or innovative format. For example, the social realist aesthetic espoused by the Third Reich is meaningful and consequential for art history, but not because examples of this art are deemed worthy of sharing the walls with the most admired works of the twentieth century; it is of interest, rather, because it was the counterpoint to (and sometimes the inspiration for) modernist works (*Entartete Kunst*) condemned by the Nazis that have became part of the modern canon.

In the following section I give examples of collective scripts fueled by the forces of discourse and distribution.

## The Script of the Familiar Narratives

As mentioned in previous chapters, the art world tends to repeat its history. Even when a work appears to be particularly new or to be radically breaking with tradition, there usually are historical precedents or parallels that show that, instead of breaking the mold, the work is a reaffirmation of the mold. I mentioned the artists who, every now and then, emerge in the art scene claiming a stake in Warhol's legacy; other artists, like Bruce Nauman, Jean-Michel Basquiat, and Ana Mendieta, similarly attract fascination, and in our constant search to find the next transformative career, we often support the careers of artists who resemble, in some ways, these forebears, hoping that we may discover a breakthrough artist or artwork of our own.

## The Script of Controversy

It may be a difficult point to accept, but sometimes art works can become historically relevant, and consequential, by mere exposure—independently of their artistic qualities. Some controversial works gained notoriety in an almost accidental fashion, by becoming symbols in a particular conflict. This was the case of *The Holy Virgin Mary*, by Chris Ofili, exhibited in 1999 at the Brooklyn Museum, which became famous for being condemned by the mayor of New York City, Rudolf Giuliani. It is arguable—although not provable—that Ofili's career would not have been propelled to the heights it has been had his work not become a cause célèbre that pitted conservative politicians against the New York art world.

It may be difficult to distinguish artworks that become controversial because of their radical aesthetics from those that become controversial by triggering a strong response from a particular social group. This is because of the complicated nature of the art controversy. Artists who find themselves in the middle of such controversies, and who may or may not have been actively seeking to create them, soon find that the debates they trigger are very distant from concrete aspects of the work or the action itself; in other words, controversies tend to become about larger issues, such as freedom of expression, or disagreements around a particular issue. When such controversy develops, the work itself usually recedes into the background, becoming a representative symbol of a contested idea. In an additional complexity, controversy carries the ring of the familiar narratives of the avant-garde, which tell us, almost in a fable-like way, that many major works of art (Duchamp's *Fountain*, Picasso's *Les Demoiselles d'Avignon*, and so forth) were highly controversial when they first became public, thus creating the false conclusion, led by the recognition of familiar narratives, that any work that provokes a controversy must carry, in the long term, an equal degree of relevance to art history.

A combination of these factors (visibility, critical mass, and less commonly, controversy) usually gives an artwork or an artist a presence in the discourse sufficient to cause an impact among local (or international) art production and, ultimately, give it a place in art-historical narratives.

It is important to emphasize that the dynamic I have described here questions the common wisdom that the art we regard most highly is the same art that eventually becomes best known. "Best art" is an impossible-to-define category. When Seyoum opened her first exhibition, it was not of great importance how sophisticated or compelling her work was, because it was presented against a blank background—that is, in a place where visitors couldn't compare it to other, similar works. By existing in a distribution environment (even if she created it for itself), it became relevant and memorable, as did the project I presented in Asunción.

I hope it may be clear from this characterization that the simple ubiquity of an art work in the art world is not enough for it to gain critical traction: in contrast to commercial products, which target as many buyers as possible, the establishment of a particular artist or art work primarily depends of the buy-in of the higher spheres, the tastemakers who set the standard of what we should collectively invest in—financially, culturally, symbolically. To appeal to the members of this sphere, there has to be a process of "conversion," by which each individual tastemaker accepts the narrative that the work or the artist is the inevitable answer to a current debate taking place in the art world. Studying the careers of certain contemporary artists—Matthew Barney, for instance—demonstrates that this process of narrative construction and conversion is a collaborative effort by individuals in different areas of the art world, who together consider the work worth defending. In Barney's case, in the early nineties, when he was a recent graduate of Yale, there were three influential figures in the art world who more or less simultaneously bought into his work: dealer Barbara Gladstone, Richard Flood (who served as director of Gladstone Gallery and later became chief curator of the Walker Art Center, in Minneapolis), and Michael Kimmelman, then chief art critic of the *New York Times*, who, after several years of favorable reviews in that paper, in 1999 wrote an article entitled "The Importance of Matthew Barney," giving him the title of the "most important artist of his generation."\* This three-part support group (art market, museum and media), added to the fact that it was solidly founded on an artist with an unusually singular body of work and an already impressive string of achievements (a show at SFMOMA, the cover of *Artforum*), helped

---

\* Michael Kimmelman, "The Importance of Matthew Barney," *New York Times*, October 10, 1999.

cement a reputation that eventually led to definitive institutional recognition—for example, a solo exhibition at the Guggenheim in 2003, in which the artist's entire Cremaster cycle was presented.

It is hard to conceive that Barney—the intrinsic value of his work, aside (as I have written in previous chapters, it is not relevant here)—could have achieved this level of institutional recognition had he not been supported by the collaborative framework described above. Today, it is extremely rare for an artist to jump to institutional recognition without having become visible, and almost ubiquitous, through a collective performance, led by discourse and distribution, by the actors listed above and communicated in the art media.

---

Symbolic interactionists (such as Blumer and Becker) argue that social actors, due to their immersion in their particular social reality, cannot entirely detach from their value commitments in their interactions. As the coordinates of distribution and discourse shape our actions, and as they reinforce or contradict the values we subscribe to, we are likely to perform along—or against—the narratives they propose, not being open to assuming or becoming convinced by new values. Unless we entirely reject the scripts (and thus exit the art scene altogether), we cannot be immune to them; we have to respond to them in the terms they enact. An example of this, which some in the art world no doubt find exasperating, is the way in which major biennials or exhibitions set a tone for discussion. Documenta and the Venice Biennale, for example, have this capacity. Once their massive curatorial statements are made, there is little more one can do than set up a position for or against them.

    I started this chapter with an example of a single artist starting a self-contained art scene in her hometown. In this case, the artist was able to build her art scene from scratch, writing a script herself. In other cases, members of the contemporary art world construct art scenes in places that have their own art traditions, thus entering into a conflict between the hegemonic art world and the local arts tradition. I observed an example of this in Mérida, Yucatán, in 2006. Mexico City artist Mónica Castillo was invited to direct the program of a school of art in Mérida. Castillo, who has a sophisticated knowledge of contemporary art, exposed the students to conceptual, performance, and process-based art, among other things. For the students, this was explosive and mind-altering; predictably, they started producing works influenced by that external discourse. But the city has a strong artistic tradition of its own—what could be called folk art—and its citizens did not understand or accept the students' projects. This caused frustration among the students, who wanted to make work that would insert itself into the international discourse, which was remote and invisible, while their immediate local viewers altogether rejected their conceptual explorations. The students, in other words, had become converts to a particular script, but they were confounded because they were performing it in a distribution vacuum.

This brings me to the larger point that the various roles we perform risk becoming meaningless when we perform them in a contextual void. Duchamp's *Fountain*, displayed in the street, is just a urinal in the street, not an artwork. As Warhol said in 1965, *we* are the art, and so we need to make sure that we are contained within an art scene, the environment that provides us with the oxygen of meaning. The metascript of distribution is the extended play within which we enact our roles, and without it we are faced with the world outside of art, which normally is not too friendly to those eccentric actors often referred to as "art types."

---

A characteristic aspect of the art scene is that we generally fulfill scripts, as interpretive performances, without knowing how to question the scripts themselves. Even when we believe that we are engaging in a process of questioning, that, too (as part of the artistic script), is part of the scene.

In the 1998 movie *The Truman Show*, the main character doesn't know that the entire world he inhabits is artificial. When he attains that realization—he has the Novalis moment of dreaming that he is dreaming, and thus awakes—he is suddenly liberated, moving into the "real" world. The ultimate irony of the movie, which we know because we see it from the outside, is that the "real" world Truman is moving into is still a movie.

The history of twentieth- and twenty-first-century art could be understood through that concatenation of moments of awareness, of those doors that artists and others open that allow us to "step out" of the reality we are living in. But the art world, in itself, the place where these realizations take place—Danto's "atmosphere of aesthetic theory" that validates but also contains the totality of our actions and statements in art—is a meta-scene, one we can't entirely escape from. Even when we become aware of its trappings, we can't figure out where exactly the frame lies and how we can step outside of it. We can certainly renounce it altogether—say, deciding to stop making art and taking on another activity—but to renounce in that way implies surrender, the understanding that we are incapable of living in that world on our own terms. So most of us, those who are not able to entirely resign from an art scene, remain with the conundrum of reluctantly performing our role within it. And while we do so, we may see the need to fulfill our roles within the parameters of the pre-established scripts because we can't figure out how to rewrite the script on our own. But the script may already be in the process of being rewritten, as I will discuss in the next section.

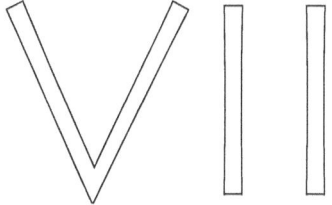

# Rewriting the Script

## The Rise of the Art User

One of the most stubborn philosophical paradoxes in art today is the fact that we, as art actors, would like art to affect the world in a tangible way, beyond the mere representation of ideas; yet when we abandon the representational realm and integrate ourselves into the world, we have stopped making art. The avant-garde of the early twentieth century happily called for the dismantling of every single attribute of art it could get rid of, inching closer, every time, to equating life with art; yet, when it had seemingly entirely rid art of all its unique attributes—with the sole exception of the name "art"—it was still not prepared to altogether eliminate the category from the repertoire of human experience. Certainly there is something important to salvage from the idea of art, and we seem to recognize that. Yet we are constantly unsatisfied by seeing artworks relegated to their own sphere, and we refuse to believe that art can't be made in a way that is consequential to the world. Whether it is due to our nostalgia for revolution, our idealism, or our incessant desire to make our activities both meaningful and practical, we continue fighting for this possibility.

In the social terms I have been utilizing throughout this book, the problem manifests as follows: we have difficulty stepping out of our "in frame" characters within the art scene in which we exist. We often attempt to break away from it, but if we want to maintain a dialogue with the art world—that is, keep ourselves inserted into "the discourse"—sooner or later we have to come to terms with it. We are, in other words, attempting to maintain "in-art-world frame" and "out-of-art-world frame" characters simultaneously.

Artists at the forefront of dealing with this problem are those who make what we today term as socially engaged art. By the very nature of that specialization, these artists have to contend with keeping one foot in the discourse of art and the other in the realm of everyday life.

Socially engaged art emerges precisely from the recognition of the social scripts of the art world, and from a desire to affect them. The social context that gives meaning to art started to be acknowledged by artists in the sixties. The process was very logical: after getting rid of the physical components of the artwork, the thing left to work on was the social environment that surrounded it. Joseph Beuys wanted to create discursive exchanges that he termed social sculpture; Marcel Broodthaers appropriated the institutional language of the museum. What came next, in the post-Minimal era—including work influenced by identity politics, feminism, and, later on, relational aesthetics—were conceptual, performative, or process-based experiences that pay a lot of attention to our roles acting as ourselves—think of Dan Graham's *Performer/Audience/Mirror* lecture (1975) and Adrian Piper's video *Cornered* (1988).

Artists in the socially engaged realm present their proposals with an exasperation that comes of not being able to break character without breaking with art altogether, and with a desire to take performativity to a level of interaction that is not merely symbolic but actual.

At this moment, the objective is no longer to critique the social scripts of art but, instead, to rewrite them. Yet, whenever we make an implicit or explicit effort to deviate from existing scripts or from an important attribute that is essential to the character we play, we face a great deal of skepticism from those around us. For example, we have become so familiar with irony in art that to take an earnest stance is deemed overly sentimental or romantic. Abandoning the central attribute of our postmodern character—the skeptical, ironic, noncommittal enfant terrible—represents going "out of frame" and thus a stoppage in play rather than a changing of the game.

Similarly, socially engaged art takes the language of critical pedagogy, liberation theology, pragmatism, and other like schools of thought in order to alter the role of the artist. This type of art is also often referred to as "social practice"; those working with communities in this capacity carefully avoid or uncomfortably sustain the label "artist," likely because of the class association that the term carries. In language closer to that of the social worker or urban planner, artists minimize the historical associations of their practice with the illuminated genius or visionary. However, it is impossible for the artist to completely renounce his or her role as author, because to do so would be not only an act of disengagement but also a relinquishing of responsibility.\*

This conundrum is similar to the difficulties faced by the playwright. In a naturalist play, the characters need to more or less conform in their reactions and behavior to a prescribed range, dictated by social conventions. Whenever the writer makes a character perform in ways that are too out of the ordinary, the play begins to seem unconvincing. For that reason, a successful play is imaginative while at the same time maintaining a consistent internal logic.

Every society alters its social codes and behavior in a long-term process that includes collective beliefs, biases, and interests. But because of the size and complexity of the art world today and the internal logic of its connected scenes, it is highly improbable that a conscious concerted effort could form to alter its social scripts from within (that is, from the place of any of the existing characters), as the scripts are ingrained in our thoughts and actions.

When the play has come to a standstill and the characters have reached an impasse in the action, the most logical resolution is the entry of a new character. I will

---

\* I discuss this point in more detail in my book *Education for Socially Engaged Art* (New York: Jorge Pinto Books, 2011).

refer to this character as the art user. But first I must speak about its predecessor, the audience member.

The art scene has a fourth wall of sorts; it presents itself to the world as a larger-than-life setting in which a drama unfolds (look, for example, at the various and highly romanticized Hollywood depictions of famous artists, ranging from Jackson Pollock to Frida Kahlo). The art scene includes a script for the casual participant or spectator of this drama, usually known as the dilettante, participant, or audience member. But today, when everyone can produce videos, blogs, and photo albums and distribute them through social networks, there is no longer a clear division between spectators and producers.

In his brief text *The Emancipated Spectator*, Jacques Rancière addresses this eroding division, arguing, "We have not to turn spectators into actors. We have to acknowledge that any spectator already is an actor of his own story and that the actor also is the spectator of the same kind of story."* He ends his essay with this now well-known statement:

> Artists, just as researchers, build the stage where the manifestation and the effect of their competences become dubious as they frame the story of a new adventure in a new idiom. The effect of the idiom cannot be anticipated. It calls for spectators who are active as interpreters, who try to invent their own translation in order to appropriate the story for

---

* Jacques Rancière, *The Emancipated Spectator* (London: Verso, 2009), p .17.

themselves and make their own story out of it. An emancipated community is in fact a community of storytellers and translators.*

Rancière describes a participant who is more active than the old passive audience member, but his "emancipated spectator" is still firmly rooted in the receiving side of things; artists are still the builders of the stage and the framers of the story in the new idiom. But a problem arises when the act of interpretation is put on the same creative level as the act of art-making.

Certainly, interpreting, narrating, and reading have elements of a creative act. But to place the interpretive act at the same level as the artistic act presents a number of uncomfortable questions: if to interpret a work is as aesthetically compelling as making it, shouldn't famous art critical writings be exhibited in museums? One could argue that all artworks are commentary on and interpretations of past artworks. But it could also be argued that artworks are not dependent on the conversation initiated by the works that inspired them. Perhaps, then, the distinction is about the degree of autonomy the artistic commentary has, whichever form it ends up taking. Perhaps Rancière does not mean to understand the spectator's rising ability to become an autonomous reader and interpreter of art at the same level as the act of art-making, but if that were to be the case, then the kind of emancipation one can attain from art would never

---

* *Ibid.*, p. 22.

be complete — as it would be permanently dependent of something to translate or reinterpret, but not an original story to originate on their own.

In their book *Consuming People: From Political Economy to Theaters of Consumption*, A. Fuat Firat and Nikhilesh Dholakia address the problem of breaking the hegemony of the market and allowing a "theater of consumption of life" to emerge: "To avoid co-optation by the market, alternatives have to develop within permeable but distinct enclaves that allow a free flow of people in and out, but maintain an autonomy from mainstream market culture."*

Socially engaged art as a practice is very much aware of its conflicting position inside the art world. Artists who work on the social realm often face the conundrum of either embracing a system that draws them toward commodification, or instead claim their own autonomy and then end up rejecting the one system that gives coherence to their way of working. However, I believe that in its philosophy, it aspires, ultimately, to create the conditions for group autonomy—for the creation of a new class of people: art users. Usually the unequivocal proof that a socially engaged art project has succeeded is that it truly provokes autonomy in a particular community, which eventually makes the experience its own and uses the knowledge gained to build new things—whether they are artistic gestures or not. The ideal ultimate scenario is one in which the artist no longer solicits the community he or

---

\* A. Fuat Firat and Nikhilesh Dholakia, *Consuming People: From Political Economy to Theaters of Consumption*. (London: Routledge, 1998) p. 157.

she aspires to transform, and the community, of its own accord, solicits the artist, or art in general, for solutions to their problems or satisfaction to their aesthetic interests.

In other words, socially engaged art inserts new actors into the play by writing a new script: one in which the art no longer is a distant or alien location for the rest of the world but is, rather, a common language, integrated into the larger cultural activity. Going beyond the platitude "Everyone is an artist," the effort to create art users promotes the existence of a new kind of individual for whom art is not a profession but rather a source of knowledge, a tool, in the same way that technology is a tool for us in reaching our various goals. In this scenario, art would be a language through which to understand the world, not just understand art itself.* The art world script would not be rewritten, but a crucial distinction would be made: art is concrete knowledge, not abstract value. Under this scenario, there would be no need to tear down museums; in the script, connoisseurship of the object would make room for connoisseurship of experience. The question remains as to what this (truly) alternative art scene, *or* alternative to the art scene, would look like.

---

* I explored and discussed this idea at length as part of the educational program I developed for the 8th Mercosul Biennial, which is presented in the anthology *Pedagogia no Campo Expandido*, Monica Hoff and Pablo Helguera, eds. (Porto Alegre, Brazil: Fundaçao Bienal do Mercosul, 2011).

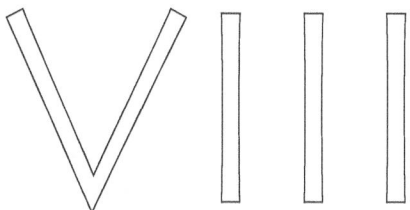

# Alternate Endings

## (The Art Scene Doubled)

> *I am not one of those who believe that civilization has to change in order for the theater to change; but I do believe that the theater, utilized in the highest and most difficult sense possible, has the power to influence the aspect and formation of things: and the encounter upon the stage of two passionate manifestations, two living centers, two nervous magnetisms is something as entire, true, even decisive, as, in life, the encounter of one epidermis with another in a timeless debauchery.*
>
> —Antonin Artaud, *No More Masterpieces*, from *The Theater and Its Double* (1938)

I have tried to describe the process of valuation in the art world through the performance of interpretive acts. I have also argued that we willingly submit to pre-established character scripts that undergo slight variations as they adapt to the coordinates of distribution and discourse. I then tried to show that, paradoxically, it is difficult for the art world insider to transform his or her own role and its script, but that, in keeping with the normal transformation of our conceptions of the role of art in society, today's scripts are being transformed by the emergence of a new actor that is a hybrid between the spectator and the artist, who understands art-making and its products not as a specialty but as a common language. I would like to conclude with an initial, if highly schematic, reflection on the conditions under which those new theaters of consumption are emerging, along with characters such as the art user, and how they might exist in relation to contemporary art's established commercial and institutional frameworks.

One important script of the art scene that I have not yet discussed in this book is the script of alternativity. Although I believe most of us know it very well, it still may be useful to review it. It goes more or less like this: a set of ideas, values, and practices is established in the art world, represented by individuals, their works, and those who vouch for them. They become widely recognized, chronicled, narrated, studied, and taught; then, a new group of individuals—usually the following generation, whose members came of age under the reign of these ideas, values, and practices, start contesting the status quo, proposing their own set of ideas, values, and practices. They construct an "alternative" art scene. As they fight to have their voices heard and their works seen, and they gradually gain more recognition; slowly they start to prevail in the contested territories of distribution and discourse. The older generation retreats and gives its place to this alternative generation, which forms the new status quo. The art world has absorbed the new generation into the establishment, but the process of integration paradoxically comes with a neutering of its original spirit. Those alternative artists have become the establishment, and they will soon be challenged by a new group of newcomers who will question their ideas.

The script of alternativity reflects the normal dynamics of the counterculture in today's world: that which claims to be against the mainstream, is in fact just waiting in the wings for its own turn at center stage. In the art world, this process is openly acknowledged, and to a regular art world participant it is not surprising, for example, that the exhibitions and artists included in a so-called alternative space can hardly be differentiated from those showing at kunsthalles or contemporary art museums.*

As I mentioned before, acting the part of the rebellious artist only reconfirms the art scene's "tradition of rupture." This creates the conundrum for an artist of being an actor who, regardless how he or she acts, will always somehow conform with what is expected; there are only mainstream or alternative—or "mainstream-at-large" (eventually to be established) artists.

Under these conditions, any attempt to truly innovate within the existing structures of the art world will not

---

* For more elaboration of the notion of alternativity and the role of the event, see the Appendices of this volume.

be viable in the long run. Moreover, given the historical investment in the narratives of modernism, it doesn't make much sense to waste energy in trying to change them. Such attacks tend to be half-hearted and ultimately contradictory. Artists, for example, who condemn the old ways as bourgeois and irrelevant (as Antonin Artaud, whom I quote in the epigraph to this chapter, does in his essays in *The Theater and Its Double*), have always stopped short of actively trying to erase that history; eventually they become part of that history themselves.

What is needed is the development of a truly alternative theater for the consumption of art—a theater in which we are more liberated from roles we are expected to fulfill. But the question remains, what to do when you can't change a system from within, but you can't completely reject it altogether, because you are still somewhat dependent on its framework?

Buckminster Fuller said, "You never change things by fighting the existing reality. To change something, build a new model that makes the existing model obsolete." While this is a useful departure point, it would be optimistic, if not naïve, to think that we could find an alternative that would render the art market obsolete. It is highly unlikely that the art market will cease to exist. However, the construction of a new theater of consumption does not necessarily entail the dismantling of the contemporary art market. For several years now the art world has slowly been branching out to create new, shadow networks of production that don't always intersect with the collecting world—the university circuit, for example, and, more extreme, work that is primarily located on the Web. So it is not impossible to conceive that not only is constructing a new theater of consumption possible, but that, in fact, many such attempts for alternatives are already in progress.

More often than attempts to replace the existing system, we see the creation of a series of "doubles"—of parallel social systems in which the idea of art remains but is reinterpreted in ways that allow for the creation of new scripts. Nearly one hundred years ago, in 1914, Spanish writer Miguel de Unamuno hinted at this idea. Annoyed by the conservative critics of his time, who charged that he was not writing novels in the appropriate manner, he claimed that he wasn't writing *"novelas"* (the Spanish word for novels) at all, but rather *"nivolas"* (his own invented word). In other words, when condemned for breaking the rules of a game, Unamuno thought, it is better to change games.

When Artaud refers to the theater's "double," he is speaking of that unconscious component of theater that contains a darker, but perhaps more urgent, truth about society than its visible and more compliant side. Interpreting Artaud's metaphor very liberally—and perhaps a bit perversely—we can say that the doubling of the art scene may not complement it, nor replace it, nor cure the establishment of art as we know it. We can no longer expect to transform art this way, just as we can't expect to eradicate religion.

What I term as the gestation of a "doubling" of the art scene has to do with our desire to rewrite the script of alternativity by writing an altogether new play and building an altogether new theater. The problem, so far, is that we can't get used to abandoning art as we knew it, nor can we fully accept that we won't be allowed back into the old scene.

So far, we have enacted brief assaults on the art establishment through the creation of temporary projects—that is, those with a self-imposed time of death that therefore cannot be eventually co-opted by the mainstream. The shifting of the emphasis to events rather than spaces is of key importance for this purpose. We could define this strategy as "making art-at-large."

Also, we know that creating projects that function equally and simultaneously in the realm of art and in other disciplines helps disrupt the natural evolution of alternativity into mainstream. Those two unique qualities of the new art practices today—their relationship to the ephemeral and their ability to operate in metamorphic ways, preventing them from being pinned down as one single thing—may be some of the attributes that will lead to the reimagined art scene of the future.

In *Ulysses*, Stephen Dedalus rhetorically asks, "What is a ghost?" and answers, "One who has faded into impalpability through death, through absence, through change of manners." This "change of manners" may be the key to our new interpretive performances. But instead of turning into ghostly imitations of ourselves, we may learn to inhabit a double, and that may result in being more real—ultimately leading us to making art less about acting and more about living.

# APPENDICES

# Alternative Time and Instant Audience

## (The Public Program as an Alternative Space)*

**1**

Spaces hold objects; they also facilitate experiences. However, physical location is only one of the factors that play a role in the production of an experience. Experience—whether art-related or not—emerges in the conjunction of a location, an event—a temporal space—and a social context, or social space. The perhaps intuitive, and appropriate, rationale for the creation of the alternative space model in the sixties and seventies was that it was necessary to have a physical location from which to present and support emerging and alternative art practices, and the same may be true today. Nonetheless, as art and the art world have evolved and as alternative art spaces have struggled to redefine their identities, too much emphasis has been given to location and too little to other key components of their character. I believe that the clue to that redefinition lies not in the reinvention of

---

* This text, with the exception of a few edits, was originally published in the anthology *In Ours, and the Hands that Hold Us: Playing by the Rules: Alternative Thinking/Alternative Spaces* (New York: apexart, 2010).

their physical space, but in paying attention to those other two factors: temporal and social context, or, in other words, events and audiences. In its updated configuration, it is increasingly clear that if any component of the alternative space could be disposed of, it is precisely its physical location—but not the social or temporal context in which it roots itself. (The same is true, in fact, of more traditional spaces: a vernissage is so central to an exhibition because spaces have become event centered, points of encounter where a particular community interacts.)

There is an inherent contradiction in the original concept of an alternative space: while it promotes an experimental, ever-evolving type of art-making, its grounding in physical location is about permanence, more about continuity or longevity than change. Furthermore, as much as a physical space can be an asset, it can also be a liability. For most alternative spaces, the struggle for financial survival is a constant threat to their programming independence; real estate, maintenance, and overhead costs can be deciding factors in their existence and can limit their flexibility. This apparent contradiction exists, perhaps, because over the years we have become too used to thinking of an alternative space as an alternative location, instead of *a* location in which to show and think about art—which, I believe, was the original impulse.

As mentioned earlier, in the late sixties, seventies, early eighties, groups of artists in New York created alternative spaces to support experimental practices that at the time did not have a home. This was long before artists, curators, and dealers had to worry too much about real estate, but also before a number of events transformed the art world, including the global explosion of art fairs and biennials, the increasing youth of artists exhibiting at major museums, the emergence of an art market thirsty for innovation, and the aggressive and experimental nature of commercial but status-seeking galleries. Today, partially as a result of the impact of those events, a regular viewer would be hard-pressed to see the difference between an exhibition or the artists showing at an alternative space and one at the New Museum of Contemporary Art in New York or at a for-profit cutting-edge exhibition space in the city. Ironically, galleries, kunsthalles, and contemporary art museums find themselves in a race to become more alternative, constantly finding ways to emulate the sound and smells of alternativity; they usually have better funding and attract talented individuals who can help facilitate the institutionalization of alternativity. Alternative art spaces are generally not for profit and lack vast resources, and, if anything, in a city like New York, they struggle to compete, with fewer resources, at games for which others are better equipped.

So are alternative spaces today truly "alternative"? Contrary to what the name may imply, alternative spaces rarely offer a real alternative to art shown elsewhere. Instead, they are inextricably connected to the critical and economic fabric of the art world. By retaining their original name, alternative spaces create the semblance of mini-subcultures, but they actually function more like clearinghouses of emerging artistic talent, providing artists room to experiment in the early stages of their careers rather than representing countercultural or underground movements. The phenomenon is not limited to New York: alternative spaces all over the world generally function in that in-between place of experimenting at the fringes while remaining in dialogue with the art world at large. While this is a valid function, we should ask if it is enough to legitimize their claim of a role as a true conceptual and practical counterpoint in the art system. I believe it is not.

When we ask about the revision of the alternative space in order to reclaim its original purpose of free experimentation and infusion of new blood into the art system, we need to look at the potential of temporality and social space. When Marcel Broodthaers invented his itinerant *Musée d'Art Moderne, Département des Aigles*, he was creating an alternative space, one that was both nomadic and temporal and which existed only in the time and place that the appropriate conditions allowed. The project would not have made sense if it had been created to last forever—that would have automatically erased its original critique of the institution.

Temporality is always part of the equation of alternativity. It is not just in a space but also at the conjunction of a particular place at a particular time that meaningful moments occur in art-making. This concept is today understood by many artists and curators, and we see more and more alternative spaces that set a temporal limit with an official date of death, which provides closure and, curiously, makes these spaces look more like large art projects. In New York, Orchard (2005–08) was an example, a temporary gallery in the Lower East Side, as was the X Initiative (2009–10), a year-long temporary space. Similarly, many spaces nowadays operate in terms of public programming and less in the terms of two-month exhibitions. Curators like Hans Ulrich Obrist have for some time explored the notion of duration-based exhibitions, such as *Il Tempo del Postino*, which Obrist presented with Philippe Parreno at Art Basel in 2009. Temporal limits provide artists, curators, and entrepreneurs with additional benefits, which include the possibility of conceiving the art space as a self-contained art project; of exploring the potential of aggressive and dynamic programming that could not be sustained in a permanent way; and of capturing the imagination and expectation of an audience who could witness the birth, climax, and death of the project. Finally, temporal limits artificially, but effectively, predetermine a historical arch for a project: alternative spaces, like every other organization, movement, or social group, experience periods of gestation, growth, climax, and decay, until their final dissolution or until they evolve into a different type of organization.

While the public program cannot replace a physical space, the fact that time is the modifier of the space and not the other way around demands a rethinking of how we produce an art experience for an audience. In cities like Los Angeles and Chicago, event-based spaces are the natural response to the awareness that, as our world moves faster and faster, alternativity is about instant communities, about the spontaneous encounter between people. Today, time is our real estate, and learning how to use it productively is as important, and perhaps even more important, than how we use the four walls of a gallery.

## 2

Public programming may be the realm in which alternativity can grow, but to simply offer public programs does not necessarily reflect, in itself, an experimental approach. The question to answer is, what sort of experimental qualities should these public programs have in order to make them most interesting or open new doors of discussion and experience? This is similar to asking what kind of experimental art will become successful, which is ultimately impossible to answer in an intelligent way. Nonetheless, based on my observations during many years of programming as educator and artist, I believe there are commonalities in experimental programming.

Content-based public programs generally fall within two distinctive genres: art-centered events, such as performances, and education-centered events, such as discussions, lectures, courses, and workshops. In my experience, the most recent innovative approaches to programming have emerged from an informed conjunction of the two, along with non-content components—such as food, drinks, and a party atmosphere—that emphasize a sense of communion.\* This has to do with the balance between program function and audience expectations. A public education program

---

\* I mentioned this phenomenon in a symposium I organized at the Museum of Modern Art, New York, titled *Transpedagogy: Contemporary Art and the Vehicles of Education*, May 15, 2009.

has the implicit function of providing a constructive experience by means of a discussion, an instructional dynamic such as the one of a workshop, or simple exposition (a straightforward lecture), and this is more or less the expectation of those who attend ("entertainment" is usually not the primary expectation among people attending a lecture, but "personal advancement" and "learning" are more likely to be). An art-based public program, in contrast, rarely offers such a structured delivery of information, growth, or learning, but it provides a direct experience that can result in all these but that is generally expected to be unmediated and direct.

An audience at an education lecture delivered by a poor speaker or a symposium in which the speakers veer off on a tangent that has nothing to do with the announced topic leave frustrated because their expectations of having a particular topic addressed in a new or informative or thoughtful way were not met.

Experimental public programs function somewhere between delivering and upsetting expectations—that is, between challenging and rewarding the viewer or the participant. Borrowing a page from performance art, these programs engage participants in entering situations with a greater degree of ambiguity, which may include things like role-playing, enacting certain social rituals (like singing in a church, wearing a costume, etc.), and sharing personal aspects of themselves (this has been often identified with the Bakhtin term, "carnivalesque"). At the same time, through pedagogical structures such as the universally understood constructs of "workshop" or "group retreat," participants are given the possibility of framing their experiences within a constructive model that allows for reflection and discussion in the future.

These experimental public programs cannot, and should not, aspire to *be* art or education; rather, those are their mediums. More than a balance between informal and formal education, this type of experimental programming is closer to informal conceptual art and informal education with a formal social agenda.

How to achieve that balance is a site-specific question, one that directly relates to how the organizers understand their own audiences.

## 3

For some, to ask who the audience will be for a new and radical art or idea appears to be a contradiction: if the art or idea is radically new, isn't it true that the audience for it doesn't exist yet? Under this logic, new ideas—or new types of art—create their own audiences. I would argue that the truth however, is different. These ideas, and those new types of art, are built for an implicit audience.

In the 1989 movie *Field of Dreams*, an Iowa farmer (played by Kevin Costner) walking through a cornfield suddenly hears the voice of God saying, "If you build it, he will come." He envisions a baseball field, and is strongly compelled to build it.

The phrase (in the variation, "If you build it, they will come") has entered the English language as if it were an old adage of ancient wisdom and not from the pen of a

Hollywood screenwriter. The implied message is: Building comes first, audiences second. Yet the opposite is true. We build *because* audiences exist. We build because we seek to reach out to others, and others will come initially because they recognize themselves in what we have built. After that initial interaction, spaces start a process of self-identification, ownership, and evolution based on group interests and ideas. They are not static spaces at which static viewers arrive, but rather ever-evolving, growing, or decaying communities that self-build, develop, and eventually dismantle.

Various sociologists have argued—David Berreby, most notably—that in most of our actions as humans we are predisposed express a tribal mindset of "us and them," and each statement we make reaches out with or against a set of pre-existing social codes that include or exclude sectors of people. Contemporary art practice, of all human endeavors, is most distinctively about exclusion, not about inclusion, because the structure of social interactions within its confines are based on a repertory of cultural codes, or "passwords," that determine a certain status and role within a given conversation. And in a radical, countercultural, or alternative practice, preserving these exclusionary passwords is key in maintaining a distance from the mainstream.

Theoretically, alternative spaces are open to all kinds of people, but they tend to serve very specific types of audiences. Smaller and more informal spaces have the flexibility to be more direct about their constituency, and they generally operate within two registers: their

immediate circle of participants and supporters, and the critical art world at large, toward which they usually look for validation. Larger alternative art spaces, because they usually are nonprofit organizations, are officially open to all, but in practice they serve a niche market within the art world: up-and-coming art professionals, individuals who are somewhat informed and interested in contemporary art, and, with lesser emphasis, more established artists and curators. Random visitors can walk into the space, but their presence or visitation is not crucial to the survival of the organization—it merely counts as foot traffic. What is key is the sustained supporter who may become a member or help raise the reputation of the space in the social fabric of the art world. Some spaces, such as Art in General in New York, have sought to diversify their audiences more aggressively, by creating neighborhood-oriented events and focusing on the ethnic groups that live near the space. In some cases, even successfully, visual artists are commissioned for residency projects working with these audiences. While these initiatives are valid and often result in interesting art projects, they run the risk of limiting the support they can provide to an artist by prescribing set parameters of audience and space and trying to fulfill quotas set by grant-making bureaucracies.*
Spaces in this situation often find themselves between a rock and a hard place, trying to sell a very hermetic product—very self-referential, cutting-edge art—to people in a

---

\* On one occasion, for a project I was invited to create for a neighborhood museum, it was stipulated that I had to engage ten ESL adult students as collaborators in the making of the work, but the expectation was that the work would be museum quality.

working-class neighborhood with very different interests and concerns.

All this is to say that alternativity, when it comes to audiences, is an unhelpful adjective. Audiences are never "others"—they are always very concrete selves. In other words, it is impossible to create an alternative experience and take steps to make it public without also making an assumption about what kinds of people will eventually partake in it. Do they read *Artforum*? Do they watch CNN? Are they English speakers? Do they live in Idaho? Did they vote for Obama? When we organize and promote an exhibition or create a public program, we are already making decisions regarding its hypothetical audience or audiences, even if just intuitively. Sociolinguist Allan Bell coined the term "audience design" in 1984, referring to the ways in which the media address different types of audiences through "style shifts" in speech.* Since that time, the discipline of sociolinguistics has defined structures by which we can recognize the patterns by which speakers engage with audiences in multiple social and linguistic environments through register and social dialect variations. This is to say that if an arts organization is to be thought of as a "speaker," it is possible to conceive it operating—through its programs and activities—in multiple social registers that may or may not include an art "intelligentsia," a more immediate contemporary art audience with its own codes and references, and the larger public.

---

\* See Allan Bell, *Language Style as Language Design*, in *Socioliguistics: A Reader and Coursebook*. Nikolas Coupland and Adam Jaworski, ed. Houndmills, Basingtoke, Hampshire: Palgrave, 1997) p. 232.

When I articulate this view, most curators and artists express weariness at the notion of a preconceived audience. To them, it sounds too restrictive and prone to mistakes. It is true that to pre-establish a demographic and a social group is to oversimplify its individuality and idiosyncrasies. At the same time, I usually turn the question the other way around—is it possible to *not* conceive of an audience, to create an experience that is intended to be public without the slightest bias toward a particular kind of interlocutor, be it a rice farmer in Laos or a professor of philosophy at Columbia University? The debate may boil down to art practice itself, and to the commonplace statement of many artists that they don't have a viewer in mind while making their work—in other words, that they only produce for "themselves." What is usually not questioned, however, is how that very notion of "ourselves" has come about. Our self is the construct of a vast collectivity of people who have influenced our thoughts and our values, and to speak "to our self" is more than a solipsistic exercise; it is a silent way of speaking to the portion of civilization that is summarized in our brain. It is true that no audience construct is absolute—they all are, in fact, fictional groupings that we make based on biased assumptions. Nonetheless, they are what we have to go by, and experience in a variety of fields has proven that, as inexact as audience constructs may be, it is more productive to work with them than blindly or obstinately act on ultimately subjective presuppositions.

The problem lies not with whether to reach for either larger or more selective audiences, but rather in understanding for ourselves our own definitions of those groups we wish to speak to, and in making conscious steps to reach out to them in a constructive and methodical way. In this regard, an alternative space that attempts to find alternative audiences doesn't benefit by trying experimental methods—it could be better served by traditional marketing. And this would not be possible unless organizers are clear with themselves in articulating the audience to whom they wish to speak.

## 4

The conjunction of temporality, community, and space, and its creative combinations, are, of course, not enough. The larger question that lies within the foundation of most alternative spaces today is the *why* of their making, their raison d'être. Ultimately, what makes an organization, a group, or even a single artist become consequential and contribute to the greater cultural dialogue is not its structural effectiveness but the resonance of its artistic or philosophical message.

If the primary motivation for an experimental practice is status seeking, the transparency of such a search becomes quite evident. What makes these spaces alive is the vibrancy of the ideas, the idealism of their founders, and the underlying political, cultural, or social cause for which they fight through concrete actions—be it exhibitions, happenings, programs, or marketing or political campaigns. This underlying motivation is what fuels the innovation of formats. And it, again, brings us back to the notion of temporality, or rather, timeliness. The public program and the instant community as alternatives to the alternative space offer the advantage that within their brief lives they can embrace their raison d'être more emphatically; like performance art, they are not rooted in permanence. Spaces, on the other hand, have to evolve; many of them can't, and some devolve and suffer painful deaths. A public program lives a short and happy life, affirming the integrity and individuality of art and ideas, without the need to multiply or be given an artificial, extended, afterlife.

# Variations on an Audience*

Ladies and Gentlemen:

Audiences are endangered species. They are slowly vanishing in this world showered with limelight, where fifteen minutes of fame is now a cacophony of 24/7 programming. We all speak at the same time, and no one listens. When everyone is an artist, no one can be in the audience. We only sit offstage because we are waiting for our turn at the lectern.

What we call an audience today, like the one here tonight, is nothing more than a collection of highly individualized minds. You all are authors, we all produce things: you take pictures, you write blogs, you all own creative real estate. You all here tonight are so different from each other. How can I, or anyone, talk to you in a comprehensive manner, so that you all feel engaged?

Unfortunately, most people who lecture have failed to recognize this simple fact. They still speak to audiences as if they existed as one whole, as if this hypothetical and amorphous mass was a homogenous group of listeners, not a heterogeneous entity of speakers. They talk to this

---

* This performance lecture, designed to be performed only once with no documentation other than this written script, was presented at the Bruce High Quality Foundation University in New York on October 13, 2009.

hypothetical audience as if it thought and felt exactly like them.

Let's take, for instance, Slavoj Žižek. Slavoj Žižek talks to everyone as if we all were Slavoj Žižek. A scholar assumes we all are scholars interested in long bibliographies and in the reference to that 1974 book where the footnote of the footnote clarifies what the footnote of the footnote of the 1973 version didn't clarify.

Artists, when they are invited to speak, usually think that their audience wants them to act as if they don't care about them, but of course artists care, and their audiences—well, their audiences usually are other artists who are respectful enough, but what they really want is not to be in the audience but to be the artist who is speaking.

So it is very painful for me to say this, but the truth is that in this post-postmodern world, we all are confused about when to speak and when to listen. As a result of this, we are both unprofessional speakers and unprofessional audiences.

This spells slight doom, the temporary boredom we all have to live through every time we attend a lecture. We don't even know why we do it. But it shouldn't be that way.

Lectures could be like sex. They could be like the seduction of love, like the erotic dance or the magic act or the psychic séance or the hypnotic session. All it takes is for the speaker to find a way to talk to each one of the persons in the room as if it were a one-to-one conversation—an audience whisperer.

So by all means, then, let's do variations on an audience, or rather, on this non-audience. I will talk not to all of you, but to each of you. For this exercise I will assume that, among the group here there is at least one person of the following sort:

1. *Theorists.* That is public intellectuals, post-structuralist scholars, downtown East Village, readers of *October* magazine.

2. *Chelseaspeakers.* Uber-professional art speakers, curators, consultants, critics.

3. *Grant-writers and administrators.* Working for nonprofit organizations and the U.S. government and the Department of Education or School Board.

4. *"Show-me-the-money" speakers.* No-nonsense, uncomplicated, like when we talk about art late at an after party after a few drinks.

Now that we have established the four sets of individuals that I will be addressing, I will now repeat my introduction in these four ways, starting with the Speaker version 1 style:

The construct of the spectator as redefined today by post-technological networks reunites a number of given implications that, upon close examination, reveal society—and its involutionary transformation—as a product of a demystified late-capitalist model without centers and reformulated contents.

The involution of cultural communication into a system of seemingly original producers of knowledge, as opposed to receivers, creates a different activity universe that contrasts with the deflection of speech, a seemingly anti-political task of horizontal results. Where one searches for the hidden receiver finds instead the manifested materialization of parallel mimetic producers. It is the fabrication of the plot of the content, the substance of normative principles of inclusion of concepts, that varies only in stylistic practices of scientific postmodernity, usually not self-identified as such but actively embracing a regiment of exclusionary concept definitions within a well-founded domain of references visible only to reduced agents of the operation.

Speech Version 2:

The notion of audience has been redefined today by post-technological networks. Cultural producers today produce works that critique Western notions of collective spectatorship and propose new critical models.

Notions of performance are incorporated in this new critique, resulting in innovative explorations that operate in the realm of conceptual art in various formats. The viewer becomes an active participant in the work, which explores notions of viewers becoming active participants.

The work becomes an active participant in the viewer, which is an exploration of notions of viewers. These works are conceptual narratives that question a variety of concepts, including the way in which spectators receive information in a postmodern world. These practices thus become explorations of conceptual information of notions of participants that participate in notions of information of conceptual explorations.

In other words, Speech Version 3:

Audiences in our global world today face the challenges and the opportunities that come along with the emerging forms of expression. In this multicultural and multidisciplinary society, there are multiple voices that reflect our diverse culture and that are important to support. In some cases, these voices will challenge the viewer to reflect on important issues we all face, but they all reflect the feelings and thoughts of others and are representative of the diversity of original community voices that we all should strive to support. We only face, as a society, the challenge to expand our long-term partnerships and advisory support to those who have an important message to convey to their constituents, building enduring foundations for community partnerships with real solutions. By acting together, we can overcome the obstacles that for too long have prevented real change on the critical issues that audiences face in art and in life, fulfilling the long objective of change, creativity, and achievement for the generations to come.

Speech Version 4:

I mean it's like sometimes because you are online so much and you get to like get to do all this like blogs and apps and movies and stuff its like today everything is so easy to do so why do we need anyone else doing it but us, like today things maybe have become retarded or something when you really think about it it's really amazing like everything can mean anything because anyone can do whatever. I mean like today the world and like culture has become a place where we all talk about ourselves and then it like makes everything look the same because no one seems to be listening or something. I mean that's cool, but it's like if I am talking and you are talking and he is talking and then if we just talk in different ways that doesn't mean we are saying different things if you know what I am saying. It's like that is how it's done today when we just say what we have to say and we know why we say it and we know what you are going to say so what's the point of even saying it, but the point that there is no point is maybe like the point.

And now, to merge these styles, we will patch together the choir of art world voices. You can call it an audience fugue:

**The construct of the spectator as redefined today by post-technological networks reunites a number of given implications that, upon close examination,** *I mean it's like sometimes because you are online so much and you get to like get to do all this like,* audiences in our global world today face the challenges and the opportunities that come along with the emerging forms of expression. The notion of audience has been redefined today by post-technological networks—**and its involutionary transformation**—as a product of a demystified late-capitalist model without centers and reformulated contents. The involution of cultural communication into a system of seemingly original producers of knowledge *it's like today everything is so easy to do so why do we need anyone else doing it but us,* In this multicultural and multidisciplinary society Cultural producers today produce works that critique western notions of collective spectatorship as opposed to receivers **creates a different activity universe that contrasts with the deflection of speech,** *blogs and apps and movies and stuff, like* there are multiple voices that reflect our diverse culture and that are important to support, *today things maybe have become retarded or something when you really think about it it's really amazing* **like a seemingly anti-political task of horizontal results.** In some cases, these voices will challenge the viewer to reflect on important issues we all face, where one searches for the hidden receiver finds instead **the manifested materialization of parallel mimetic producers** but they all reflect the feelings and thoughts of others and are representative of the diversity of original community voices that we all should strive to support, *I mean everything can mean anything because anyone can do, like, whatever.* **It is the fabrication of the plot of the content,** *I mean like today the world and like,* **the substance of normative principles of inclusion of concepts,** that we only face as a society the challenge to expand our long-term partnerships and advisory support to those who have an important message to convey to their constituents, These works are conceptual narratives that question a variety of concepts, *where we all talk about ourselves and then it like makes everything look* *the same because no one seems to be listening or something.* By acting together, we can overcome the obstacles that for too long have prevented real change on the critical issues that audiences face in art and life, **only in stylistic practices of scientific postmodernity,** *I mean that's cool, but it's like if I am talking and you are talking and he is talking and then if we just talk in different ways that doesn't mean we are saying different things, like* These practices thus become explorations of conceptual information of notions of participants, building enduring foundations for community partnerships with real solutions, **usually not self-identified as such but actively embracing a regiment of exclusionary definitions that** participate in notions of information of conceptual explorations, *if you know what I am saying,* **including the way in which spectators receive information in a postmodern world,** *and we know why we say it and we know what you are going to say so what's the point of even saying it,* **within a well-founded domain of references visible only to a reduced agents of the operation,** fulfilling the long objective of change, creativity, and achievement for the generations to come, an exploration of notions of viewers, *Its like that is how its done today when we just say what we have to say but the point that there is no point is maybe, like, the point.*

## OTHER TITLES BY THE AUTHOR

*Endingness: Prolegomena for a New Art of Memory*
*The Pablo Helguera Manual of Contemporary Art Style*
*The Witches of Tepoztlán (and Other Unpublished Operas)*
*The Boy Inside the Letter*
*Artoons (I, II & III)*
*The Juvenal Players*
*Suite Panamericana*
*Estela y las Hojas*
*Theatrum Anatomicum (and Other Performance Lectures)*
*What in the World*
*The School of Panamerican Unrest: An Anthology of Documents* (with Sara Demeuse)
*Urÿonstelaii*
*Onda Corta*
*Education for Socially Engaged Art (A Materials and Techniques Handbook)*

PABLO HELGUERA (born in Mexico City in 1971) is a visual and performance artist. Some of his past art projects have included a phonographic archive of dying languages, a memory theater, fourteen visual artist "heteronyms," and four fictional opera composers. In 2006 he drove from Anchorage to Tierra del Fuego with a collapsible schoolhouse, organizing discussions, activist happenings, and civic ceremonies along the way (*The School of Panamerican Unrest*). He has been the recipient of Creative Capital, Guggenheim, and Franklin Furnace fellowships, and in 2011 he was the first recipient of the International Award for Participatory Art, given by the Assembly of Emilia-Romagna, in Italy. In 2011 he was pedagogical curator of the 8th Mercosul Biennial in Porto Alegre, Brazil. Since 2007 Helguera has been Director of Adult and Academic Programs in the Department of Education at the Museum of Modern Art, New York. He is married to artist Dannielle Tegeder, and they live in Brooklyn with their daughter, Estela.

www.ingramcontent.com/pod-product-compliance
Lightning Source LLC
Chambersburg PA
CBHW031923240526
45464CB00022B/648